The Beginner's Guide to
JavaScript

: An Essential Introduction to Coding for Web
Development, Interactive Sites, and Beyond

Matthew D.Passmore

Table Of Content

Introduction

Welcome to "Beginner's Guide to JavaScript: An Essential Introduction to Coding for Web Development, Interactive Sites, and Beyond." This book is designed to guide you through the fundamentals of JavaScript, one of the most popular and versatile programming languages in web development. Whether you are completely new to coding or have some experience with other languages, this guide will provide you with the knowledge and skills you need to start building dynamic and interactive web applications.

JavaScript powers the interactive elements on web pages, from simple form validations to complex animations and single-page applications. Its flexibility and ease of integration with HTML and CSS make it an essential tool for any aspiring web developer.

In this book, we'll start with the basics, such as setting up your development environment and writing your first JavaScript program. From there, we'll delve into more advanced topics like control flow, functions, and working with the Document Object Model (DOM). We'll also cover modern JavaScript features, best practices, and introduce you to popular frameworks that can further enhance your web development capabilities.

By the end of this book, you'll have a solid understanding of JavaScript and be well-equipped to create engaging and functional web applications. Let's embark on this exciting journey into the world of JavaScript together!

Setting Up Your Development Environment

Before diving into JavaScript coding, it's essential to set up a development environment that will allow you to write, test, and debug your code efficiently. A well-configured environment can significantly enhance your productivity and ease the learning process.

1. Choose a Code Editor

A good code editor is your primary tool for writing JavaScript. Here are some popular options:

Visual Studio Code (VS Code): A powerful, open-source code editor with a rich ecosystem of extensions for JavaScript development.

Sublime Text: A lightweight and fast editor with excellent syntax highlighting and support for many programming languages.
Atom: An open-source editor developed by GitHub, known for its customizable interface and strong community support.

2. Install Node.js

Node.js is a JavaScript runtime that allows you to run JavaScript code outside of a browser. It also includes npm (Node Package Manager), which is useful for managing libraries and dependencies.

Download Node.js: Visit the Node.js website and download the installer for your operating system.
Install Node.js: Run the installer and follow the instructions. The installation process will include npm.
To verify the installation, open a terminal or command prompt and run the following commands:

```sh
Copy code
node -v
npm -v
```

These commands should display the installed versions of Node.js and npm.

3. Setting Up a Project Folder

Create a dedicated folder for your JavaScript projects. This will help keep your files organized. You can name the folder anything you like, for example, javascript-projects.

4. Installing a Web Browser

Modern web browsers come with powerful developer tools that are indispensable for JavaScript development. Google Chrome and Mozilla Firefox are popular choices due to their robust debugging features.

5. Configuring the Code Editor

Once you have chosen a code editor, you can enhance its functionality with extensions and plugins. Here are some recommended extensions for Visual Studio Code:

ESLint: Integrates the ESLint JavaScript linter into VS Code to help you write error-free code.
Prettier: A code formatter that ensures your code follows consistent style guidelines.
Live Server: Launches a local development server with live reload feature for static and dynamic pages.

6. Version Control with Git

Version control is crucial for managing changes to your codebase. Git is the most widely used version control system. Here's how to set it up:

Install Git: Download and install Git from the official website.
Configure Git: Set up your Git username and email in the terminal:

sh
Copy code
git config --global user.name "Your Name"

git config --global user.email "you@example.com"

7. Setting Up a Simple Web Server

For testing JavaScript code that interacts with HTML and CSS, you might want to set up a simple web server. You can use the http-server package, which you can install using npm:

```sh
Copy code
npm install -g http-server
```

To run the server, navigate to your project folder in the terminal and execute:

```sh
Copy code
http-server
```

This will start a local web server, and you can access your project in a web browser at http://localhost:8080.

Conclusion

With your development environment set up, you're ready to start coding in JavaScript. A well-organized workspace and the right tools will make your learning journey smoother and more enjoyable. In the next chapter, we'll begin with the basics of JavaScript and write your first program. Let's get started!

Overview of JavaScript in Web Development

JavaScript is a cornerstone technology in web development, alongside HTML and CSS. While HTML structures the content of web pages and CSS styles it, JavaScript brings interactivity and dynamism, transforming static pages into engaging user experiences. Understanding its role and capabilities is crucial for any aspiring web developer.

The Role of JavaScript

JavaScript was initially created to add interactive elements to web pages, such as form validations, animations, and dynamic content updates. Over the years, its role has expanded significantly, and it now powers a wide range of functionalities:

Client-Side Scripting: JavaScript runs in the browser, allowing developers to create responsive interfaces that react to user actions without needing to reload the page. This is essential for creating modern web applications.

Server-Side Scripting: With the advent of Node.js, JavaScript can also run on the server, enabling developers to use a single language for both client-side and server-side code.

Full-Stack Development: JavaScript frameworks and libraries like React, Angular, and Vue.js for front-end development, and Node.js with Express for back-end development, allow for building entire web applications using JavaScript.

Key Features of JavaScript

JavaScript boasts several features that make it a powerful and versatile language:

Event-Driven Programming: JavaScript can respond to events such as user clicks, form submissions, and page loads, making it ideal for creating interactive web applications.

Asynchronous Programming: With features like callbacks, promises, and async/await, JavaScript can handle asynchronous operations efficiently, crucial for tasks like fetching data from APIs without blocking the user interface.

Prototypal Inheritance: Unlike traditional class-based object-oriented languages, JavaScript uses prototypal inheritance, allowing objects to inherit properties and methods directly from other objects.

Dynamic Typing: JavaScript is a dynamically typed language, meaning variables can hold values of any type without needing explicit declarations.

JavaScript in the Browser

JavaScript's primary environment is the web browser. Every major browser (Chrome, Firefox, Safari, Edge) includes a JavaScript engine that executes JavaScript code:

DOM Manipulation: JavaScript can access and modify the Document Object Model (DOM), which represents the structure of an HTML document. This allows developers to change the content, structure, and style of web pages dynamically.

Event Handling: JavaScript can listen for and respond to various user interactions, such as clicks, key presses, and mouse movements, making web pages interactive.

APIs: Browsers provide various APIs (Application Programming Interfaces) that JavaScript can use to perform tasks like making network requests (Fetch API), storing data locally (Local Storage), and interacting with multimedia content (Canvas API).

Popular JavaScript Libraries and Frameworks
To streamline development and enhance capabilities, numerous libraries and frameworks have been built around JavaScript:

jQuery: A fast, small, and feature-rich library that simplifies tasks like DOM manipulation, event handling, and Ajax.
React: A library for building user interfaces, particularly single-page applications, using a component-based architecture.
Angular: A comprehensive framework for building dynamic web applications, developed and maintained by Google.
Vue.js: A progressive framework for building user interfaces, known for its simplicity and flexibility.

The Future of JavaScript

JavaScript continues to evolve, with regular updates bringing new features and improvements. The ECMAScript (ES) specification, the standard upon which JavaScript is based, ensures that the language keeps pace with modern development needs. Recent versions have introduced features like arrow functions, template literals, and modules, making JavaScript more powerful and easier to work with.

Conclusion

JavaScript is an indispensable tool in web development, enabling the creation of dynamic, interactive, and feature-rich web applications. As you progress through this book, you will gain a deep understanding of JavaScript's core concepts and learn how to leverage its capabilities to build robust web solutions. Whether you're interested in front-end, back-end, or full-stack development, mastering JavaScript is a crucial step on your journey. Let's explore the exciting world of JavaScript and unlock its full potential!

Chapter 1
Getting Started with JavaScript

Welcome to the exciting journey of learning JavaScript! As one of the core technologies of the web, alongside HTML and CSS, JavaScript enables you to create dynamic and interactive user experiences. Whether you're new to programming or looking to expand your skills, this chapter will lay the groundwork for your JavaScript learning journey.

We'll begin with the essentials, helping you understand what JavaScript is and why it is so important in modern web development. You'll learn how to set up your environment, write your first lines of JavaScript code, and see how it interacts with HTML to enhance web pages. By the end of this chapter, you'll have a solid foundation to build upon as you delve deeper into JavaScript and unlock its full potential. Let's get started!

Understanding the Basics of JavaScript

JavaScript is a lightweight, interpreted language that runs in web browsers. It enables developers to create dynamic content that can respond to user actions, manipulate the DOM (Document Object Model), and communicate with servers without requiring page reloads.

Key Features of JavaScript

Interactivity: JavaScript can react to user actions such as clicks, hovers, and keyboard inputs, making web pages interactive and engaging.

Dynamic Content: JavaScript allows you to update the content of a web page without reloading it, enhancing user experience.

Asynchronous Programming: Using techniques like callbacks, promises, and async/await, JavaScript can handle tasks such as fetching data from APIs without freezing the user interface.

Cross-Browser Compatibility: JavaScript runs on all major web browsers, making it a universal tool for web development.

Embedding JavaScript in HTML

JavaScript can be embedded in HTML in three main ways:

Inline JavaScript: You can include JavaScript directly within an HTML element's attribute. For example:

html
Copy code
```
<button onclick="alert('Hello, world!')">Click Me</button>
```

Internal JavaScript: You can place JavaScript code within <script> tags inside the HTML document:

html
Copy code
```
<!DOCTYPE html>
<html lang="en">
<head>
  <meta charset="UTF-8">
  <title>Internal JavaScript</title>
</head>
<body>
  <h1>Hello, World!</h1>
```

```
<script>
    document.querySelector('h1').textContent = 'Hello,
JavaScript!';
  </script>
</body>
</html>
```

External JavaScript: For better organization and reusability, you can write JavaScript in separate .js files and link them to your HTML document:

html
Copy code

```
<!DOCTYPE html>
<html lang="en">
<head>
  <meta charset="UTF-8">
  <title>External JavaScript</title>
  <script src="script.js"></script>
</head>
<body>
  <h1>Hello, World!</h1>
</body>
</html>
```
javascript

Copy code
```
// script.js
document.querySelector('h1').textContent    =    'Hello,
JavaScript!';
```

Basic Syntax and Concepts

Variables: Variables store data values. You can declare variables using var, let, or const:

javascript
Copy code
```
let message = 'Hello, World!';
const pi = 3.14159;
```

Data Types: JavaScript supports various data types, including numbers, strings, booleans, objects, and arrays:

javascript
Copy code
```
let number = 42; // Number
let name = 'Alice'; // String
let isActive = true; // Boolean
let user = { name: 'Alice', age: 25 }; // Object
let numbers = [1, 2, 3, 4, 5]; // Array
```

Operators: JavaScript includes arithmetic, comparison, and logical operators:

```javascript
Copy code
let sum = 5 + 3; // Arithmetic
let isEqual = (5 === 5); // Comparison
let isBothTrue = (true && true); // Logical
```

Functions: Functions encapsulate reusable code blocks:

```javascript
Copy code
function greet(name) {
    return `Hello, ${name}!`;
}
console.log(greet('Alice'));
```

Control Structures: JavaScript uses control structures like if, for, and while to direct the flow of the program:

```javascript
Copy code
if (number > 10) {
    console.log('Number is greater than 10');
```

```
}

for (let i = 0; i < 5; i++) {
  console.log(i);
}

let count = 0;
while (count < 5) {
  console.log(count);
  count++;
}
```

Conclusion

Understanding these basics of JavaScript will enable you to start building dynamic and interactive web pages. As you progress, you'll learn more advanced concepts and techniques that will allow you to create more sophisticated applications. Let's continue our journey and deepen our knowledge of this powerful language!

Embedding JavaScript in HTML

Embedding JavaScript in HTML allows you to enhance web pages with interactivity and dynamic content. There are three primary methods to embed JavaScript into HTML: inline JavaScript, internal JavaScript, and external JavaScript. Each method has its use cases and benefits, which we'll explore in this section.

Inline JavaScript

Inline JavaScript is placed directly within an HTML element's attribute. This method is useful for adding simple interactivity, such as handling a button click or a form submission.

Example:

```html
Copy code
<!DOCTYPE html>
<html lang="en">
<head>
  <meta charset="UTF-8">
  <title>Inline JavaScript</title>
</head>
<body>
```

```html
    <button onclick="alert('Hello, world!')">Click Me</button>
</body>
</html>
```

In this example, the onclick attribute of the <button> element contains a JavaScript function that displays an alert when the button is clicked.

Internal JavaScript

Internal JavaScript is written within <script> tags inside the HTML document. This method is useful for embedding JavaScript code that applies to the specific page, allowing you to keep your code organized within the same file.

Example:

html
Copy code
```html
<!DOCTYPE html>
<html lang="en">
<head>
    <meta charset="UTF-8">
    <title>Internal JavaScript</title>
```

```
<script>
    function changeText() {
        document.getElementById('myText').textContent =
'Hello, JavaScript!';
    }
</script>
</head>
<body>
    <h1 id="myText">Hello, World!</h1>
    <button onclick="changeText()">Change Text</button>
</body>
</html>
```

In this example, the JavaScript function changeText is defined within the <script> tags in the <head> section. When the button is clicked, it calls the changeText function, which changes the text content of the <h1> element.

External JavaScript

External JavaScript is written in separate .js files and linked to the HTML document using the <script src="path/to/your/file.js"></script> tag. This method is ideal for organizing code, especially for larger projects, as it keeps HTML and JavaScript code separate and reusable.

Example:
HTML file (index.html):

html
Copy code

```
<!DOCTYPE html>
<html lang="en">
<head>
    <meta charset="UTF-8">
    <title>External JavaScript</title>
    <script src="script.js"></script>
</head>
<body>
    <h1 id="myText">Hello, World!</h1>
    <button onclick="changeText()">Change Text</button>
</body>
</html>
```

JavaScript file (script.js):

javascript
Copy code

```
function changeText() {
```

```
document.getElementById('myText').textContent =
'Hello, JavaScript!';
}
```

In this example, the JavaScript code is written in an external file named script.js. The HTML file links to this script using the <script src="script.js"></script> tag. When the button is clicked, the changeText function from the external file is executed.

Choosing the Right Method

Inline JavaScript: Use for very simple and quick tasks, but avoid for more complex logic as it can clutter your HTML and make maintenance difficult.

Internal JavaScript: Use for small scripts specific to a single HTML page. It keeps the code together but can still clutter the HTML if overused.

External JavaScript: Use for larger scripts and reusable code. This method promotes separation of concerns, making your code easier to manage and maintain.

Best Practices

Separation of Concerns: Prefer external JavaScript files to keep HTML clean and make your code more modular and maintainable.

Avoid Inline JavaScript: Reserve inline JavaScript for simple tasks or when absolutely necessary. Inline scripts can make your HTML hard to read and debug.

Minimize Internal JavaScript: Use internal scripts for page-specific code, but be mindful of keeping your HTML clean and organized.

Load Scripts at the End: Place <script> tags at the end of the <body> section or use the defer attribute in the <head> to ensure that the HTML content loads before the JavaScript executes.

Example of using defer:

```html
Copy code
<!DOCTYPE html>
<html lang="en">
<head>
  <meta charset="UTF-8">
```

```html
<title>Deferred JavaScript</title>
<script src="script.js" defer></script>
</head>
<body>
<h1 id="myText">Hello, World!</h1>
<button onclick="changeText()">Change Text</button>
</body>
</html>
```

By understanding and applying these methods and best practices, you can effectively embed JavaScript in HTML, enhancing the interactivity and functionality of your web pages.

Your First JavaScript Program

Writing your first JavaScript program is an exciting milestone. In this section, we'll guide you through creating a basic JavaScript application that interacts with a web page. This simple exercise will help you understand how

JavaScript works within an HTML document and introduce you to essential concepts.

Setting Up Your Environment

Before writing your first program, make sure you have the following set up:

A text editor or an integrated development environment (IDE) like Visual Studio Code, Sublime Text, or Atom.
A web browser (Google Chrome, Mozilla Firefox, etc.) to run and test your code.

Creating the HTML File

First, create a new HTML file named index.html in your text editor. This file will contain the structure of your web page and the embedded JavaScript code.

```
html
Copy code
<!DOCTYPE html>
<html lang="en">
<head>
  <meta charset="UTF-8">
```

```
    <meta name="viewport" content="width=device-width,
initial-scale=1.0">
    <title>My First JavaScript Program</title>
</head>
<body>
    <h1 id="greeting">Welcome to JavaScript!</h1>
                <button    onclick="displayMessage()">Click
Me</button>

    <script>
        // Your JavaScript code will go here
    </script>
</body>
</html>
```

In this HTML file:

The <h1> element with the ID greeting will display a welcome message.

A <button> element with an onclick attribute will call a JavaScript function when clicked.

Writing Your First JavaScript Function

Next, add a JavaScript function inside the <script> tags. This function will display an alert message when the button is clicked.

html
Copy code

```
<script>
    function displayMessage() {
            alert('Hello, world! This is your first JavaScript program.');
    }
</script>
```

Adding Interactivity

Now, let's make our JavaScript program interact with the HTML content. We'll modify the text inside the <h1> element when the button is clicked.

html
Copy code

```
<script>
    function displayMessage() {
        // Display an alert message
            alert('Hello, world! This is your first JavaScript program.');

        // Change the text content of the <h1> element
```

```
    document.getElementById('greeting').textContent =
'Hello, JavaScript!';
  }
</script>
```
In this code:

The displayMessage function uses alert to show a message box.
It then changes the text content of the <h1> element with the ID greeting using document.getElementById('greeting').textContent.

Testing Your Program

Save the File: Save your index.html file.
Open in a Browser: Open the file in a web browser by double-clicking it or dragging it into the browser window.
Interact with the Page: Click the "Click Me" button. You should see an alert message followed by the text in the <h1> element changing to "Hello, JavaScript!".

Conclusion

Congratulations! You've just written and executed your first JavaScript program. This simple exercise has demonstrated how JavaScript can interact with HTML elements and respond to user actions. You now have a foundational understanding of how to embed JavaScript in an HTML document and make web pages dynamic and interactive.

As you progress, you'll learn more about JavaScript syntax, control structures, and how to manipulate the DOM more effectively. Keep experimenting with small projects and build upon this basic knowledge to become proficient in JavaScript. Let's continue our journey and explore more advanced concepts in the next chapters!

Chapter 2
Variables and Data Types

In JavaScript, variables and data types are fundamental concepts that form the backbone of programming. Variables act as containers for storing data that can be used and manipulated throughout your code, while data types define the nature of that data. Understanding how to declare and use variables, as well as the different data types available, is crucial for writing effective and efficient JavaScript programs. In this section, we'll explore how to declare variables, the various data types you can work with, and how to choose the right type for your data. This knowledge will provide you with a solid foundation for developing dynamic and interactive web applications.

Declaring Variables

Declaring variables is a fundamental aspect of programming in JavaScript. It involves creating a named storage location in which you can store data values. This section will cover the different ways to declare variables in JavaScript, including the var, let, and const keywords, and explain their characteristics and use cases.

The var Keyword

Introduction: var was the original way to declare variables in JavaScript. It is function-scoped, meaning that a variable declared with var is available throughout the function in which it is declared.

Example:
javascript
Copy code
```
function exampleFunction() {
    var message = 'Hello, world!';
    console.log(message); // Outputs: Hello, world!
}
exampleFunction();
console.log(message); // Error: message is not defined
```

Characteristics:

Function Scope: Variables declared with var are scoped to the function in which they are declared. Outside of this function, the variable is not accessible.

Hoisting: var declarations are hoisted to the top of their scope, meaning they are accessible before their actual declaration in the code.

The let Keyword

Introduction: Introduced in ES6 (ECMAScript 2015), let provides block-level scoping, which means a variable declared with let is only accessible within the block (enclosed by {}) in which it is declared.

Example:

```javascript
Copy code
function exampleFunction() {
    let message = 'Hello, world!';
    if (true) {
        let message = 'Hello, block!';
        console.log(message); // Outputs: Hello, block!
    }
    console.log(message); // Outputs: Hello, world!
```

```
}
exampleFunction();
```

Characteristics:

Block Scope: let variables are limited to the block in which they are declared, making them more predictable and reducing potential errors in larger codebases.
No Hoisting: let variables are not hoisted to the top of their block scope; they are only available after their declaration.

The const Keyword

Introduction: Also introduced in ES6, const is used to declare variables whose values should not be reassigned after their initial assignment. Like let, const is block-scoped.

Example:
javascript
Copy code
```
function exampleFunction() {
    const message = 'Hello, world!';
    console.log(message); // Outputs: Hello, world!
        // message = 'New value'; // Error: Assignment to
constant variable
```

```
}
exampleFunction();
```

Characteristics:

Block Scope: const variables are block-scoped, similar to let.
Immutability: While the value of a const variable cannot be reassigned, objects and arrays declared with const can still have their contents modified.
No Hoisting: const variables are not hoisted and are only accessible after their declaration.

Choosing the Right Keyword

var: Use var for legacy code or when working with older JavaScript environments. Generally, var is less preferred due to its function-scoping and hoisting behavior.
let: Use let for variables that may change value and need to be limited to a specific block scope. It provides more control and reduces scope-related bugs.
const: Use const for variables that should remain unchanged after initialization. It enforces immutability, making your code more predictable and reliable.

Conclusion

Choosing the right way to declare variables—whether with var, let, or const—is crucial for writing clear and maintainable JavaScript code. Understanding the differences between these keywords and their appropriate use cases will help you manage variable scope and behavior effectively.

Understanding Data Types

In JavaScript, data types are fundamental concepts that define the kind of data that can be stored and manipulated. Understanding these data types is crucial for writing effective code and handling data correctly. JavaScript is a dynamically typed language, meaning variables can hold values of any data type and can change types during runtime. Here's an overview of the primary data types in JavaScript:

Primitive Data Types
Number

Description: Represents both integer and floating-point numbers. JavaScript does not distinguish between different numeric types; all numbers are treated as floating-point values.

Example:
javascript
Copy code
```
let age = 25;     // Integer
let price = 19.99;  // Floating-point
```

Characteristics:

Can be used in arithmetic operations.
Includes special values like Infinity and NaN (Not-a-Number).
String

Description: Represents sequences of characters used to store and manipulate text. Strings can be enclosed in single quotes, double quotes, or backticks (template literals).

Example:
javascript
Copy code

```javascript
let firstName = 'Alice';
let greeting = "Hello, world!";
let template = `Hello, ${firstName}!`;
```

Characteristics:

Strings are immutable, meaning their values cannot be changed once created.
Supports various methods for manipulation, such as .length, .toUpperCase(), and .substring().

Boolean

Description: Represents a logical value that can be either true or false.

Example:

```javascript
javascript
Copy code
let isActive = true;
let isLoggedIn = false;
```

Characteristics:

Often used in conditional statements and loops to control the flow of execution.

Undefined

Description: Represents a variable that has been declared but not yet assigned a value. It is the default value for variables that are not initialized.

Example:
javascript
Copy code
let x;
console.log(x); // Outputs: undefined

Characteristics:

Indicates that a variable exists but has not been given a specific value.

Null

Description: Represents the intentional absence of any object value. It is used to explicitly indicate that a variable should have no value.

Example:

javascript

Copy code

```javascript
let y = null;
console.log(y); // Outputs: null
```

Characteristics:

Different from undefined, as null is assigned intentionally to signify the absence of value.

Symbol

Description: Represents unique and immutable values that can be used as object property keys. Symbols are useful for creating unique identifiers.

Example:

javascript

Copy code

```javascript
let uniqueId = Symbol('description');
```

Characteristics:

Symbols are unique and cannot be duplicated.

Useful for creating unique object property keys.

Non-Primitive Data Types

Object

Description: Represents complex data structures that can hold collections of data in key-value pairs. Objects can store multiple values in a single variable.

Example:
javascript
Copy code
```javascript
let person = {
   name: 'Bob',
   age: 30,
   isStudent: false
};
```

Characteristics:

Objects are mutable, meaning their properties can be added, modified, or deleted.
Supports methods and can be used to create more complex data structures.

Array

Description: Represents ordered collections of values. Arrays can store multiple values in a single variable and can contain values of different types.

Example:
javascript
Copy code
```javascript
let numbers = [1, 2, 3, 4, 5];
let fruits = ['apple', 'banana', 'cherry'];
```

Characteristics:

Arrays are zero-indexed, meaning the first element is at index 0.
Supports various methods for manipulation, such as .push(), .pop(), and .map().

Conclusion

Understanding JavaScript's data types is essential for managing and manipulating data effectively in your programs. Knowing the differences between primitive and non-primitive types, and how to use each type, will help you write more accurate and efficient code. With this foundational knowledge, you'll be well-equipped to handle a wide range of programming tasks and challenges in JavaScript.

Working with Numbers, Strings, and Booleans

In JavaScript, numbers, strings, and booleans are fundamental data types used to represent and manipulate data. Understanding how to work with these types effectively is crucial for performing calculations, handling text, and controlling the flow of your programs. This section explores how to work with each of these data types, including their operations, methods, and common use cases.

Working with Numbers

JavaScript handles numbers as floating-point values, allowing for both integer and decimal calculations. Here's how to work with numbers in JavaScript:

Basic Operations:

```javascript
Copy code
let a = 10;
let b = 5;
console.log(a + b); // Addition: 15
console.log(a - b); // Subtraction: 5
console.log(a * b); // Multiplication: 50
console.log(a / b); // Division: 2
console.log(a % b); // Modulus: 0 (remainder of division)
```

Special Values:

Infinity: Represents positive or negative infinity.

```javascript
Copy code
console.log(1 / 0); // Infinity
console.log(-1 / 0); // -Infinity
```

NaN (Not-a-Number): Represents a value that is not a valid number.

```javascript
Copy code
console.log(0 / 0); // NaN
```

console.log(parseInt('hello')); // NaN

Number Methods:

toFixed(): Formats a number to a specified number of decimal places.

```javascript
Copy code
let num = 123.456;
console.log(num.toFixed(2)); // Outputs: 123.46
```

toString(): Converts a number to its string representation.
```javascript
Copy code
let num = 100;
console.log(num.toString()); // Outputs: "100"
```

Working with Strings

Strings in JavaScript are sequences of characters used for text manipulation. Here's how to work with strings:

String Operations:

javascript
Copy code
```
let str1 = 'Hello';
let str2 = 'World';
console.log(str1 + ' ' + str2); // Concatenation: "Hello World"
```

String Methods:

length: Returns the number of characters in a string.
javascript
Copy code
```
let str = 'JavaScript';
console.log(str.length); // Outputs: 10
```

toUpperCase() and toLowerCase(): Convert a string to upper or lower case.

javascript
Copy code
```
let str = 'Hello World';
console.log(str.toUpperCase()); // Outputs: "HELLO WORLD"
console.log(str.toLowerCase()); // Outputs: "hello world"
```

substring() and slice(): Extract parts of a string.

javascript

Copy code

```
let str = 'JavaScript';
console.log(str.substring(0, 4)); // Outputs: "Java"
console.log(str.slice(4)); // Outputs: "Script"
```

Template Literals: Allow for easier string interpolation and multi-line strings.

javascript

Copy code

```
let name = 'Alice';
let greeting = `Hello, ${name}!`;
console.log(greeting); // Outputs: "Hello, Alice!"
```

Working with Booleans

Booleans represent logical values: true and false. They are used in control flow and conditional statements to determine the execution of code blocks.

Basic Operations:

javascript

Copy code

```
let isAdult = true;
let isStudent = false;
console.log(isAdult && isStudent); // Logical AND: false
console.log(isAdult || isStudent); // Logical OR: true
console.log(!isAdult); // Logical NOT: false
```

Common Use Cases:

Conditional Statements: Used to control the flow of the program.

javascript
Copy code

```
let age = 18;
if (age >= 18) {
    console.log('You are an adult.');
} else {
    console.log('You are not an adult.');
}
```

Comparison Operators: Used to compare values and return boolean results.

javascript

```
Copy code
let x = 10;
let y = 20;
console.log(x == y); // Equality: false
console.log(x < y); // Less than: true
console.log(x !== y); // Not equal: true
```

Conclusion

Mastering how to work with numbers, strings, and booleans is essential for effective JavaScript programming. By understanding their operations and methods, you can handle calculations, manipulate text, and control program flow efficiently. These fundamental data types are the building blocks of more complex operations and data structures, so a solid grasp of their use will greatly enhance your programming skills.

Chapter 3
Operators and Expressions

In JavaScript, operators and expressions are core elements that allow you to perform calculations, compare values, and control the flow of your programs. Operators are symbols that perform operations on one or more operands, while expressions are combinations of variables, values, and operators that evaluate to a single result. Understanding how to use operators and construct expressions is crucial for writing effective and efficient code.

This section will introduce you to the various types of operators available in JavaScript, including arithmetic, comparison, logical, and assignment operators. You'll learn how to use these operators to create meaningful expressions, manipulate data, and implement logic in your programs. By mastering operators and expressions, you'll be able to build more dynamic and interactive applications.

Arithmetic Operators

Arithmetic operators in JavaScript perform basic mathematical operations on numbers. These operators are essential for calculations and numerical manipulations in your code. Here's a breakdown of the primary arithmetic operators and how they are used:

Basic Arithmetic Operators
Addition (+)

Description: Adds two operands together.
Example:
javascript
Copy code
```javascript
let a = 5;
let b = 10;
let sum = a + b; // sum is 15
```
Subtraction (-)

Description: Subtracts the second operand from the first.

Example:
javascript
Copy code
```javascript
let a = 15;
let b = 5;
```

let difference = a - b; // difference is 10
Multiplication (*)

Description: Multiplies two operands.

Example:
javascript
Copy code
let a = 6;
let b = 7;
let product = a * b; // product is 42
Division (/)

Description: Divides the first operand by the second.

Example:
javascript
Copy code
let a = 20;
let b = 4;
let quotient = a / b; // quotient is 5
Modulus (%)

Description: Returns the remainder of the division of the first operand by the second.

Example:
javascript
Copy code
let a = 10;
let b = 3;
let remainder = a % b; // remainder is 1
Exponentiation (**)

Description: Raises the first operand to the power of the second operand.

Example:
javascript
Copy code
let base = 2;
let exponent = 3;
let result = base ** exponent; // result is 8 (2^3)

Operator Precedence

JavaScript follows a set order of operations known as operator precedence when evaluating expressions. Arithmetic operators have specific precedence levels that determine the sequence in which operations are performed.

For instance, multiplication and division are performed before addition and subtraction.

Example:

javascript
Copy code

```
let result = 5 + 3 * 2; // result is 11, not 16
// Multiplication is performed before addition
```

Working with Different Data Types

Strings: The + operator can also be used for string concatenation.

javascript

Copy code

```
let greeting = 'Hello, ';
let name = 'Alice';
let message = greeting + name; // message is "Hello, Alice"
```

Mixed Types: When combining numbers and strings, JavaScript performs type coercion. Numbers are converted to strings and concatenated.

javascript
Copy code

```
let num = 10;
let text = ' apples';
let result = num + text; // result is "10 apples"
```

Conclusion

Arithmetic operators are fundamental to performing calculations and manipulating numerical values in JavaScript. By understanding and effectively using these operators, you can perform a wide range of mathematical operations and create more complex and interactive functionality in your programs.

Comparison Operators

Comparison operators in JavaScript are used to compare values and determine their relationship. These operators return a boolean value (true or false) based on the result of the comparison. They are essential for controlling the flow of a program, particularly in conditional statements and loops. Here's a detailed look at the various comparison operators:

Types of Comparison Operators
Equal to (==)

Description: Compares two values for equality, performing type coercion if necessary.

Example:
javascript
Copy code
```
let a = 5;
let b = '5';
console.log(a == b); // true, because '5' is coerced to the number 5
```
Strict Equal to (===)

Description: Compares two values for equality without performing type coercion. Both value and type must be the same.

Example:
javascript
Copy code
```
let a = 5;
let b = '5';
```

console.log(a === b); // false, because 5 (number) is not strictly equal to '5' (string)
Not Equal to (!=)

Description: Compares two values for inequality, performing type coercion if necessary.

Example:
javascript
Copy code
let a = 5;
let b = '5';
console.log(a != b); // false, because '5' is coerced to the number 5 and they are considered equal
Strict Not Equal to (!==)

Description: Compares two values for inequality without performing type coercion. Both value and type must be different.

Example:
javascript
Copy code
let a = 5;
let b = '5';

console.log(a !== b); // true, because 5 (number) is not strictly equal to '5' (string)
Greater Than (>)

Description: Checks if the value on the left is greater than the value on the right.

Example:
javascript
Copy code
```
let a = 10;
let b = 5;
console.log(a > b); // true
```
Greater Than or Equal to (>=)

Description: Checks if the value on the left is greater than or equal to the value on the right.

Example:
javascript
Copy code
```
let a = 10;
let b = 10;
console.log(a >= b); // true
```
Less Than (<)

Description: Checks if the value on the left is less than the value on the right.

Example:
javascript
Copy code
```
let a = 5;
let b = 10;
console.log(a < b); // true
```
Less Than or Equal to (<=)

Description: Checks if the value on the left is less than or equal to the value on the right.

Example:
javascript
Copy code
```
let a = 5;
let b = 5;
console.log(a <= b); // true
```

Type Coercion

When using comparison operators like == and !=, JavaScript performs type coercion, converting values to a common type before making the comparison. This can sometimes lead to unexpected results, so it's often safer to use the strict comparison operators (=== and !==) to avoid type coercion issues.

Example:
javascript
Copy code
```
console.log(0 == false); // true, because 0 is coerced to false
console.log(0 === false); // false, because 0 and false are of different types
```

Practical Use Cases

Comparison operators are often used in conditional statements such as if, else if, and while to control the flow of execution based on the results of comparisons.

Example:
javascript
Copy code
```
let age = 18;
```

```
if (age >= 18) {
    console.log('You are an adult.');
} else {
    console.log('You are not an adult.');
}
.
```

Conclusion

Comparison operators are crucial for making decisions and controlling the flow of your JavaScript programs. By understanding how to use these operators and being mindful of type coercion, you can write more reliable and accurate code that correctly handles different data types and conditions.

Logical Operators

Logical operators in JavaScript are used to perform logical operations on boolean values. They are essential for combining multiple conditions and controlling the flow of your program based on complex criteria. Here's a look at the primary logical operators and how they are used:

Types of Logical Operators

Logical AND (&&)

Description: Returns true if both operands are true. Otherwise, it returns false.
Usage: Often used to ensure multiple conditions are met before executing a block of code.

Example:
javascript
Copy code
```
let age = 25;
let hasID = true;
if (age >= 18 && hasID) {
    console.log('You can enter the club.');
} else {
    console.log('Access denied.');
}
```

Logical OR (||)

Description: Returns true if at least one of the operands is true. If both are false, it returns false.

Usage: Used to check if at least one of multiple conditions is true.

Example:
javascript
Copy code
```
let isWeekend = true;
let isHoliday = false;
if (isWeekend || isHoliday) {
    console.log('You can relax today.');
} else {
    console.log('It's a workday.');
}
```

Logical NOT (!)

Description: Returns true if the operand is false, and false if the operand is true. It effectively inverts the boolean value.
Usage: Used to reverse the boolean value of a condition.

Example:
javascript
Copy code
```
let isLoggedIn = false;
if (!isLoggedIn) {
```

```javascript
  console.log('Please log in to continue.');
} else {
  console.log('Welcome back!');
}
```

Short-Circuit Evaluation

Logical operators in JavaScript use short-circuit evaluation, meaning that the evaluation stops as soon as the result is determined.

Logical AND (&&): If the first operand is false, the second operand is not evaluated because the overall result will be false.

javascript
Copy code

```javascript
function getUser() { return null; }
let user = getUser() && getUser().name; // getUser() is called only once, if at all
```

Logical OR (||): If the first operand is true, the second operand is not evaluated because the overall result will be true.

javascript
Copy code
```javascript
let username = null;
let defaultName = 'Guest';
let displayName = username || defaultName; // defaultName is used if username is falsy
```

Truthy and Falsy Values

In JavaScript, values that are not explicitly true or false can still be evaluated in a boolean context. These are referred to as truthy and falsy values:

Falsy Values: false, 0, " (empty string), null, undefined, NaN. Truthy Values: Any value that is not falsy, including non-zero numbers, non-empty strings, objects, and arrays.
Practical Use Cases
Logical operators are commonly used in conditional statements and loops to control the flow based on multiple conditions.

Example with Conditional Statements:

javascript
Copy code

```javascript
let userRole = 'admin';
let hasPermission = true;
if (userRole === 'admin' && hasPermission) {
  console.log('Access granted.');
} else {
  console.log('Access denied.');
}
```

Example with Loops:

javascript
Copy code
```javascript
let numbers = [1, 2, 3, 4, 5];
for (let i = 0; i < numbers.length; i++) {
  if (numbers[i] % 2 === 0 || numbers[i] > 4) {
    console.log(numbers[i]);
  }
}
```

Conclusion

Logical operators are a powerful tool for combining conditions and controlling the flow of your JavaScript programs. By understanding and effectively using these operators, you can create more sophisticated and flexible logic, allowing your code to handle complex scenarios and make decisions based on multiple criteria.

Working with Expressions

In JavaScript, expressions are combinations of variables, values, operators, and functions that are evaluated to produce a value. Expressions are a fundamental part of programming, as they allow you to perform calculations, manipulate data, and make decisions based on the results. Understanding how to construct and use expressions is key to writing effective and efficient code.

Types of Expressions

Arithmetic Expressions

Description: Perform mathematical operations such as addition, subtraction, multiplication, and division.

Example:

```javascript
Copy code
let a = 10;
let b = 5;
let sum = a + b;      // Arithmetic expression: 10 + 5
let product = a * b;   // Arithmetic expression: 10 * 5
```

Comparison Expressions

Description: Compare values using comparison operators and return a boolean result (true or false).

Example:
```javascript
Copy code
let x = 10;
let y = 20;
let isEqual = (x == y); // Comparison expression: 10 == 20
let isGreater = (x > y); // Comparison expression: 10 > 20
```

Logical Expressions

Description: Combine boolean values using logical operators to produce a boolean result.
Example:

javascript
Copy code

```javascript
let isAdult = true;
let hasTicket = false;
let canEnter = isAdult && hasTicket; // Logical expression: true && false
```

String Expressions

Description: Concatenate strings or perform operations involving strings.

Example:
javascript
Copy code

```javascript
let firstName = 'John';
let lastName = 'Doe';
let fullName = firstName + ' ' + lastName; // String expression: 'John' + ' ' + 'Doe'
```

Unary Expressions

Description: Operate on a single operand to produce a result, such as incrementing a value or negating a boolean.
Example:

```javascript
Copy code
let count = 5;
count++;            // Unary expression: increment count by 1
let isTrue = !false;    // Unary expression: negate false to get true
```

Compound Expressions

Description: Combine multiple expressions using operators to form more complex expressions.
Example:

```javascript
Copy code
let a = 10;
let b = 20;
let c = 30;
let result = (a + b) * c; // Compound expression: (10 + 20) * 30
```

Evaluation Order

Expressions are evaluated based on operator precedence and associativity rules. JavaScript follows a specific order when evaluating expressions:

Precedence: Determines which operators are evaluated first. For example, multiplication has higher precedence than addition.

Associativity: Determines the order of operations for operators of the same precedence level. Most operators are left-associative, meaning they are evaluated from left to right.

Example:

```javascript
Copy code
let result = 2 + 3 * 4; // Multiplication is performed before addition
// Result is 14 (2 + (3 * 4))
```

Using Expressions in Control Flow

Expressions are often used within control flow statements such as if, while, and for to determine whether certain blocks of code should execute.

Example:
javascript
Copy code
```
let age = 25;
if (age >= 18) {
    console.log('You are an adult.'); // Expression inside if condition
} else {
    console.log('You are not an adult.');
}
```

Conclusion

Expressions are a fundamental concept in JavaScript programming, enabling you to perform calculations, make comparisons, and manipulate data. By understanding how to construct and evaluate expressions, you can write more dynamic and functional code, handle complex logic, and make your programs more interactive and responsive.

Chapter 4
Control Flow

Control flow refers to the order in which individual statements, instructions, or function calls are executed or evaluated in a programming language. In JavaScript, control flow mechanisms are essential for directing the execution path of your code based on conditions, loops, and exceptions. They allow you to create dynamic and responsive programs by making decisions, repeating tasks, and handling errors.

This section will introduce the primary control flow structures in JavaScript, including conditional statements, loops, and error handling constructs. Understanding these control flow mechanisms will enable you to implement complex logic, automate repetitive tasks, and manage exceptions gracefully, leading to more efficient and robust programs.

Conditional Statements (if, else if, else)

Conditional statements in JavaScript allow you to execute different blocks of code based on specific conditions. These statements enable your program to make decisions and respond differently to various inputs or situations. The primary conditional statements in JavaScript are if, else if, and else.

if Statement

The if statement evaluates a condition (an expression that returns a boolean value). If the condition is true, the code block inside the if statement is executed. If the condition is false, the code block is skipped.

Syntax:

```javascript
Copy code
if (condition) {
    // Code to execute if condition is true
}
```

Example:

javascript
Copy code

```
let age = 18;
if (age >= 18) {
    console.log('You are an adult.');
}
```

else Statement

.

The else statement is used in conjunction with if to specify a block of code to be executed if the if condition is false. It provides an alternative path of execution when the initial condition is not met.

Syntax:

javascript
Copy code

```
if (condition) {
    // Code to execute if condition is true
} else {
    // Code to execute if condition is false
}
```

Example:

```javascript
Copy code
let age = 16;
if (age >= 18) {
    console.log('You are an adult.');
} else {
    console.log('You are not an adult.');
}
```

else if Statement

The else if statement allows you to test multiple conditions sequentially. If the initial if condition is false, the else if condition is evaluated. If the else if condition is true, its code block is executed. You can have multiple else if statements to check various conditions.

Syntax:

```javascript
Copy code
if (condition1) {
    // Code to execute if condition1 is true
```

```
} else if (condition2) {
    // Code to execute if condition2 is true
} else {
    // Code to execute if both conditions are false
}
```

Example:

```javascript
Copy code
let score = 85;
if (score >= 90) {
    console.log('Grade: A');
} else if (score >= 80) {
    console.log('Grade: B');
} else if (score >= 70) {
    console.log('Grade: C');
} else {
    console.log('Grade: F');
}
```

Nested Conditional Statements

You can nest if, else if, and else statements within each other to create more complex decision-making structures.

Example:
javascript
Copy code

```javascript
let age = 25;
let hasID = true;
if (age >= 18) {
  if (hasID) {
    console.log('You can enter the club.');
  } else {
    console.log('You need an ID to enter.');
  }
} else {
  console.log('You are not old enough to enter.');
}
```

Ternary Operator

For simple conditional assignments, you can use the ternary operator (? :), which provides a concise way to evaluate a condition and return one of two values.

Syntax:

javascript

Copy code
condition ? valueIfTrue : valueIfFalse
Example:

```javascript
Copy code
let age = 20;
let message = age >= 18 ? 'You are an adult.' : 'You are not an adult.';
console.log(message); // Output: You are an adult.
```

.

Conclusion

Conditional statements are a fundamental aspect of control flow in JavaScript, allowing you to create dynamic and responsive programs. By using if, else if, and else statements, you can direct the execution of your code based on various conditions, making your applications more flexible and intelligent. Understanding how to use these statements effectively is essential for implementing complex logic and decision-making in your JavaScript programs.

Switch Statements

Switch statements in JavaScript provide a way to execute different blocks of code based on the value of an expression. They offer a cleaner and more readable alternative to multiple if...else if statements when you need to compare a single variable against multiple possible values.

Syntax

The basic syntax of a switch statement is as follows:

javascript
Copy code
```
switch (expression) {
    case value1:
        // Code to execute if expression === value1
        break;
    case value2:
        // Code to execute if expression === value2
        break;
    // More cases as needed
    default:
```

```
    // Code to execute if none of the cases match
}
```

How it Works

Expression: The switch statement evaluates the expression once.

Case Labels: The expression's value is compared against the value of each case label. If a match is found, the corresponding block of code is executed.

Break Statement: Each case should end with a break statement to prevent the code from falling through to the next case. If the break statement is omitted, the code will continue executing the next case block, regardless of whether it matches the expression's value.

Default Case: The default case is optional but recommended. It executes if none of the case labels match the expression's value.

Example
Here's an example of a switch statement to determine the day of the week:

javascript

```
Copy code
let day = 3;
let dayName;

switch (day) {
  case 1:
    dayName = 'Monday';
    break;
  case 2:
    dayName = 'Tuesday';
    break;
  case 3:
    dayName = 'Wednesday';
    break;
  case 4:
    dayName = 'Thursday';
    break;
  case 5:
    dayName = 'Friday';
    break;
  case 6:
    dayName = 'Saturday';
    break;
  case 7:
    dayName = 'Sunday';
```

```javascript
      break;
   default:
      dayName = 'Invalid day';
}
```

```javascript
console.log(dayName); // Output: Wednesday
```

Fall-Through Behavior

If you omit the break statement at the end of a case, the execution will continue to the next case, regardless of its value. This behavior is known as "fall-through."

Example:
javascript
Copy code
```javascript
let fruit = 'apple';
switch (fruit) {
   case 'apple':
      console.log('Apples are $1.00 each.');
   case 'banana':
      console.log('Bananas are $0.50 each.');
      break;
   case 'cherry':
      console.log('Cherries are $3.00 per pound.');
```

```javascript
      break;
    default:
      console.log('Unknown fruit.');
}
// Output:
// Apples are $1.00 each.
// Bananas are $0.50 each.
```

Using Expressions in Switch Cases

Switch cases can use expressions as well, but they are evaluated strictly (using ===).

Example:
javascript
Copy code
```javascript
let grade = 'B';
switch (grade) {
  case 'A':
    console.log('Excellent!');
    break;
  case 'B':
  case 'C':
    console.log('Well done.');
    break;
```

```
    case 'D':
      console.log('You passed.');
      break;
    case 'F':
      console.log('Better luck next time.');
      break;
    default:
      console.log('Invalid grade.');
}
// Output: Well done.
```

Conclusion

Switch statements in JavaScript provide a structured and readable way to handle multiple conditional branches based on the value of an expression. By using case labels and the default case, you can efficiently direct the flow of your program. While the if...else if construct is more flexible for complex conditions, switch statements shine in scenarios where you need to compare a single value against multiple discrete options. Understanding when and how to use switch statements can help you write clearer and more maintainable code.

Looping with for, while, and do...while

Loops in JavaScript allow you to execute a block of code multiple times based on a specified condition. They are essential for performing repetitive tasks, iterating over arrays, and managing large sets of data. JavaScript provides three main types of loops: for, while, and do...while.

for Loop

The for loop is used when you know in advance how many times you want to execute a statement or a block of statements. It is often used to iterate over arrays or perform a task a specific number of times.

Syntax:

```javascript
Copy code
for (initialization; condition; increment) {
    // Code to be executed
```

}
Example:

```javascript
Copy code
for (let i = 0; i < 5; i++) {
    console.log('Iteration number: ' + i);
}
// Output:
// Iteration number: 0
// Iteration number: 1
// Iteration number: 2
// Iteration number: 3
// Iteration number: 4
```

Explanation:

Initialization: Sets a variable before the loop starts (e.g., let i = 0).

Condition: Defines the condition for the loop to continue (e.g., i < 5).

Increment: Increases the variable value after each iteration (e.g., i++).

while Loop

The while loop executes a block of code as long as a specified condition is true. It is useful when you don't know in advance how many times the loop should run.

Syntax:

```javascript
Copy code
while (condition) {
    // Code to be executed
}
```

Example:

```javascript
Copy code
let i = 0;
while (i < 5) {
    console.log('Iteration number: ' + i);
    i++;
}
// Output:
// Iteration number: 0
// Iteration number: 1
// Iteration number: 2
```

// Iteration number: 3
// Iteration number: 4

Explanation:

Condition: The loop continues as long as this condition is true (e.g., i < 5).

Code Execution: The code inside the loop runs for each iteration as long as the condition remains true.
do...while Loop

The do...while loop is similar to the while loop, but it guarantees that the code block is executed at least once before the condition is tested. This loop is useful when the code block needs to run at least once regardless of the condition.

Syntax:

```javascript
Copy code
do {
    // Code to be executed
} while (condition);
```

Example:

```javascript
Copy code
let i = 0;
do {
  console.log('Iteration number: ' + i);
   i++;
} while (i < 5);
// Output:
// Iteration number: 0
// Iteration number: 1
// Iteration number: 2
// Iteration number: 3
// Iteration number: 4
```

Explanation:

Code Execution: The code inside the do block is executed first.
Condition: The condition is checked after the code block has been executed (e.g., $i < 5$).
Infinite Loops
Be cautious with loops to avoid creating infinite loops, where the condition never becomes false, causing the loop to

run indefinitely. This can freeze your program and consume excessive resources.

Example of an Infinite Loop:

javascript
Copy code
```
while (true) {
    console.log('This will run forever!');
}
```
Breaking Out of Loops
You can use the break statement to exit a loop prematurely, based on a specific condition.

Example:
javascript
Copy code
```
for (let i = 0; i < 10; i++) {
    if (i === 5) {
        break; // Exit the loop when i is 5
    }
    console.log('Iteration number: ' + i);
}
// Output:
// Iteration number: 0
```

```
// Iteration number: 1
// Iteration number: 2
// Iteration number: 3
// Iteration number: 4
```

Conclusion

Loops are fundamental constructs in JavaScript that enable
you to execute code repeatedly based on conditions. The for
loop is ideal for a known number of iterations, the while
loop is useful for indefinite iterations based on a condition,
and the do...while loop ensures the code runs at least once.
Understanding and using these loops effectively can help
you manage repetitive tasks, iterate over data structures, and
create more efficient programs.

Chapter 5.
Functions

Functions in JavaScript are reusable blocks of code designed to perform a specific task. They allow you to structure your code efficiently, making it more readable and maintainable. A function can accept inputs (parameters) and return a value, enabling complex operations to be encapsulated within simple, callable units

Defining and Calling Functions

Functions in JavaScript are defined using the function keyword, followed by a name, a set of parentheses (), and a block of code {}. Once defined, you can call the function to execute the code within it.

Defining a Function

A basic function definition includes the function's name and a block of code that runs when the function is called.

Syntax:

```javascript
Copy code
function functionName() {
    // Code to be executed
}
```

Example:

```javascript
Copy code
function greet() {
    console.log('Hello, world!');
}
```

Calling a Function

To call a function, simply use its name followed by parentheses. This executes the code inside the function.

Syntax:

```javascript
Copy code
```

functionName();

Example:

```javascript
Copy code
greet(); // Output: Hello, world!
```

Parameters and Arguments

Functions can accept inputs, known as parameters, which are specified within the parentheses during function definition. When calling the function, you provide arguments that correspond to these parameters.

Example:

```javascript
Copy code
function greet(name) {
   console.log('Hello, ' + name + '!');
}

greet('Alice'); // Output: Hello, Alice!
greet('Bob');  // Output: Hello, Bob!
```

Returning Values

Functions can return a value using the return statement. This allows you to use the result of the function in other parts of your code.

Example:
javascript
Copy code
```
function add(a, b) {
    return a + b;
}

let result = add(5, 3);
console.log(result); // Output: 8
```

Function Expressions

Functions can also be defined using expressions, allowing them to be assigned to variables. These functions can be anonymous (without a name).

Example:
javascript
Copy code

```javascript
let multiply = function(a, b) {
    return a * b;
};
```

```javascript
console.log(multiply(4, 5)); // Output: 20
```

Arrow Functions

Introduced in ES6, arrow functions provide a shorter syntax for writing function expressions. They are particularly useful for concise functions.

Example:
javascript
Copy code
```javascript
let subtract = (a, b) => a - b;
```

```javascript
console.log(subtract(10, 4)); // Output: 6
```

Conclusion

Defining and calling functions is a fundamental aspect of JavaScript programming. By encapsulating code into reusable functions, you can make your code more modular, maintainable, and efficient. Understanding how to define, call, and utilize functions effectively is key to mastering JavaScript.

Function Parameters and Return Values

Function parameters and return values are essential concepts in JavaScript, allowing functions to accept inputs and produce outputs. These features make functions versatile and powerful, enabling you to write reusable and dynamic code.

Function Parameters

Parameters are variables listed as part of a function definition. They act as placeholders for the values that will be passed to the function when it is called.

Defining Parameters:

javascript
Copy code

```javascript
function functionName(parameter1, parameter2) {
    // Code to be executed
}
```

Example:

javascript
Copy code
```javascript
function greet(name, age) {
    console.log('Hello, ' + name + '. You are ' + age + ' years old.');
}
```

```javascript
greet('Alice', 30); // Output: Hello, Alice. You are 30 years old.
```

Function Arguments

.

Arguments are the actual values passed to the function when it is invoked. They correspond to the function's parameters.

Example:
javascript
Copy code

greet('Bob', 25); // Output: Hello, Bob. You are 25 years old.

Default Parameters

You can assign default values to parameters. If no argument is provided for a parameter with a default value, the function uses the default.

Example:
javascript
Copy code

```javascript
function greet(name = 'Guest', age = 'unknown') {
    console.log('Hello, ' + name + '. Your age is ' + age + '.');
}
```

greet(); // Output: Hello, Guest. Your age is unknown.
greet('Charlie'); // Output: Hello, Charlie. Your age is unknown.

Return Values

Functions can return a value using the return statement. This allows the function to produce an output that can be used elsewhere in your code. If a function does not have a return statement, it returns undefined by default.

Returning a Value:

```javascript
Copy code
function add(a, b) {
  return a + b;
}

let result = add(5, 3);
console.log(result); // Output: 8
```

Multiple Return Statements:

```javascript
Copy code
function checkAge(age) {
  if (age >= 18) {
    return 'Adult';
  } else {
    return 'Minor';
  }
}
```

console.log(checkAge(20)); // Output: Adult
console.log(checkAge(15)); // Output: Minor

Using Returned Values

The returned value from a function can be assigned to a variable, passed to another function, or used in expressions.

Example:
javascript
Copy code
```
function square(num) {
  return num * num;
}

let squaredNumber = square(4);
console.log(squaredNumber); // Output: 16

console.log(square(add(2, 3))); // Output: 25
```

Conclusion
Understanding function parameters and return values is crucial for writing effective JavaScript code. Parameters allow functions to accept input, making them flexible and

reusable, while return values enable functions to produce outputs that can be utilized in various parts of your program. Mastering these concepts will help you create more dynamic and efficient JavaScript applications.

Scope and Closures

Scope and closures are fundamental concepts in JavaScript that affect how variables and functions are accessed and managed within different parts of your code. Understanding these concepts is crucial for writing effective and bug-free JavaScript.

Scope
Scope refers to the visibility and lifetime of variables in different parts of your code. JavaScript has two main types of scope:

Global Scope:

Variables declared outside any function or block have global scope, meaning they can be accessed from anywhere in the code.

Example:
javascript
Copy code
let globalVar = 'I am global';

```
function showGlobal() {
    console.log(globalVar); // Output: I am global
}
```

```
showGlobal();
console.log(globalVar); // Output: I am global
```

Local Scope:

Variables declared within a function or a block (using let or const) have local scope, meaning they are only accessible within that function or block.

Example:
javascript
Copy code

```javascript
function localScopeExample() {
    let localVar = 'I am local';
    console.log(localVar); // Output: I am local
}

localScopeExample();
console.log(localVar); // Error: localVar is not defined
```

Block Scope

With ES6, JavaScript introduced block scope using let and const. Variables declared with these keywords are only accessible within the block they are defined, such as inside {}.

Example:
javascript
Copy code
```javascript
if (true) {
    let blockScopedVar = 'I am block scoped';
    console.log(blockScopedVar); // Output: I am block scoped
}
```

console.log(blockScopedVar); // Error: blockScopedVar is not defined

Closures

A closure is a feature where an inner function retains access to the variables and parameters of its outer function even after the outer function has finished executing. Closures allow functions to have "private" variables and provide powerful ways to create functions with persistent state.

Creating a Closure:

```javascript
Copy code
function outerFunction() {
    let outerVar = 'I am from outer function';

    function innerFunction() {
        console.log(outerVar); // Accesses outerVar from outerFunction
    }

    return innerFunction;
}
```

let closureFunction = outerFunction();
closureFunction(); // Output: I am from outer function
Explanation:

innerFunction is a closure because it "closes over" the outerVar variable from its enclosing scope.
Even after outerFunction has executed, innerFunction still has access to outerVar.

Practical Uses of Closures

Data Encapsulation:
Closures can be used to create private variables and functions, providing a way to encapsulate and protect data.

Example:
javascript
Copy code

```
function createCounter() {
  let count = 0;

  return function() {
    count++;
    return count;
  };
```

}

let counter = createCounter();
console.log(counter()); // Output: 1
console.log(counter()); // Output: 2

Function Factories:

Closures can be used to create customized functions with pre-configured settings.

Example:
javascript
Copy code
```javascript
function makeMultiplier(multiplier) {
  return function(number) {
    return number * multiplier;
  };
}
```

let double = makeMultiplier(2);
console.log(double(5)); // Output: 10

Conclusion

Understanding scope and closures is essential for managing variable visibility and creating flexible, maintainable code in JavaScript. Scope determines where variables can be accessed, while closures provide powerful mechanisms for creating functions with persistent states and encapsulating data. Mastering these concepts will help you write more effective and organized JavaScript code.

Arrow Functions

Arrow functions, introduced in ES6 (ECMAScript 2015), provide a concise syntax for writing functions in JavaScript. They simplify function expressions and have unique behavior compared to traditional function expressions, particularly with respect to the this keyword.

Syntax

Arrow functions use the => syntax, which makes them shorter and often more readable compared to traditional function expressions.

Basic Syntax:

```javascript
Copy code
(parameters) => {
    // Code to be executed
}
```

Example:

```javascript
Copy code
const greet = () => {
    console.log('Hello, world!');
};
```

greet(); // Output: Hello, world!

Key Features

Concise Syntax:

Arrow functions reduce boilerplate code by omitting the function keyword and using an arrow (=>) between parameters and the function body.

Example:
javascript
Copy code
```
// Traditional function
function add(a, b) {
    return a + b;
}

// Arrow function
const add = (a, b) => a + b;
```

Single Expression Return:

If the function body contains a single expression, the braces {} and return keyword can be omitted. The expression's result is automatically returned.

Example:
javascript
Copy code
```
const square = x => x * x;
```

console.log(square(4)); // Output: 16

No this Binding:

Arrow functions do not have their own this context. Instead, they inherit this from the surrounding lexical context (the context in which they were created). This is particularly useful in situations where you need to preserve the this context, such as in callback functions.

Example:
javascript
Copy code
```
function Counter() {
  this.value = 0;

  setInterval(() => {
    this.value++; // 'this' refers to the Counter instance
    console.log(this.value);
  }, 1000);
}

new Counter();
// Output: 1, 2, 3, 4, ...
```
No arguments Object:

Arrow functions do not have their own arguments object, which contains the arguments passed to a function. Instead, they access arguments from the enclosing scope if needed.

Example:

```javascript
Copy code
function showArgs() {
    const arrowFunc = () => {
        console.log(arguments); // `arguments` from the outer function
    };

    arrowFunc();
}

showArgs(1, 2, 3); // Output: [1, 2, 3]
```

Limitations

Cannot be Used as Constructors:
Arrow functions cannot be used with the new keyword, so they cannot be used as constructors.

Example:
javascript
Copy code
```javascript
const Person = (name) => {
  this.name = name;
};


const john = new Person('John'); // Error: Person is not a
constructor
```

.

No this Binding:

.

While this can be beneficial, it also means that arrow
functions cannot be used as methods in objects if you need
them to have their own this context.

Example:
javascript
Copy code
```javascript
const obj = {
  value: 10,
  getValue: () => this.value // 'this' does not refer to obj
};


console.log(obj.getValue()); // Output: undefined
```

Conclusion

Arrow functions offer a more concise syntax and resolve common issues with the this keyword in JavaScript. They are particularly useful for short functions and callbacks. However, they come with some limitations, such as the inability to be used as constructors and the lack of their own this binding. Understanding when and how to use arrow functions will help you write cleaner and more efficient JavaScript code.

Chapter 6
Objects and Arrays

In JavaScript, objects and arrays are fundamental data structures used to store and manage collections of data.

Objects: Objects are collections of key-value pairs where each key (also called a property) is a string (or symbol) and each value can be any data type. Objects are ideal for representing structured data and organizing related values under a single entity.

Example:
```javascript
Copy code
let person = {
    name: 'Alice',
    age: 30,
    greet: function() {
        console.log('Hello, ' + this.name);
    }
};

console.log(person.name); // Output: Alice
```

person.greet(); // Output: Hello, Alice

Arrays: Arrays are ordered lists of values, indexed by numbers starting from 0. They are useful for storing sequences of items and performing operations like iteration, sorting, and manipulation.

Example:

```javascript
Copy code
let numbers = [1, 2, 3, 4, 5];

console.log(numbers[0]); // Output: 1
numbers.push(6);
console.log(numbers); // Output: [1, 2, 3, 4, 5, 6]
```

Objects and arrays are versatile and widely used for handling data in JavaScript, allowing developers to create complex structures and manage collections of information efficiently.

Introduction to Objects

In JavaScript, an object is a fundamental data structure that allows you to store and manage collections of related data and functionalities. Objects are used to represent real-world entities, such as a person, a car, or a book, by grouping together properties and methods related to that entity.

Key Concepts

Definition:
An object is defined using curly braces {}, with properties and methods enclosed within. Each property is a key-value pair, where the key is a string (or symbol) and the value can be any valid JavaScript data type.

Example:
javascript
Copy code
```javascript
let car = {
    brand: 'Toyota',
    model: 'Corolla',
    year: 2021,
    startEngine: function() {
        console.log('Engine started');
    }
```

};

Properties:

Properties are the key-value pairs in an object. The key (or property name) is a string (or symbol), and the value can be a string, number, boolean, array, another object, or a function.

Accessing Properties:

```javascript
Copy code
console.log(car.brand); // Output: Toyota
console.log(car['model']); // Output: Corolla
Modifying Properties:
```

```javascript
Copy code
car.year = 2022;
console.log(car.year); // Output: 2022
Methods:
```
Methods are functions defined within an object. They allow objects to perform actions or operations related to the object's data.

Example:
javascript
Copy code

```
car.startEngine(); // Output: Engine started
```

Creating Objects:

Objects can be created in several ways:

Object Literal Notation:

javascript
Copy code

```
let person = {
    name: 'John',
    age: 30
};
```

Constructor Function:

javascript
Copy code

```
function Person(name, age) {
    this.name = name;
```

```javascript
    this.age = age;
}

let person1 = new Person('Alice', 25);
```
Object.create() Method:

```javascript
javascript
Copy code
let proto = {
  greet: function() {
    console.log('Hello');
  }
};

let obj = Object.create(proto);
obj.greet(); // Output: Hello
```

Object Properties and Methods:

Adding Properties:

```javascript
javascript
Copy code
car.color = 'red';
```
Deleting Properties:

javascript
Copy code
```
delete car.color;
```

Enumerating Properties:

javascript
Copy code
```
for (let key in car) {
   console.log(key + ': ' + car[key]);
}
```

Conclusion

Objects are versatile and powerful in JavaScript, providing a way to group related data and functions together. They form the backbone of JavaScript programming, enabling the creation of complex data structures and facilitating the organization and management of data and behavior. Understanding how to create and manipulate objects is essential for effective JavaScript development.

Working with Object Properties and Methods

In JavaScript, objects are used to group related data and functionalities. Understanding how to work with object properties and methods is crucial for effective object-oriented programming and data management.

Object Properties

Properties are key-value pairs within an object. They can hold any type of data, including primitive values, arrays, and even other objects.

Accessing Properties

You can access object properties using dot notation or bracket notation.

Dot Notation:

```javascript
Copy code
```

```javascript
let car = {
  brand: 'Toyota',
  model: 'Corolla'
};

console.log(car.brand); // Output: Toyota
```

Bracket Notation:

javascript
Copy code
```javascript
console.log(car['model']); // Output: Corolla
```

Bracket notation is useful when the property name is dynamic or not a valid identifier (e.g., contains spaces or special characters).

Adding Properties
You can add new properties to an object using dot notation or bracket notation.

Dot Notation:

javascript
Copy code

car.year = 2022;
Bracket Notation:

```javascript
Copy code
car['color'] = 'blue';
```

Modifying Properties
Existing properties can be modified by simply reassigning their values.

Example:
```javascript
Copy code
car.model = 'Camry';
```

Deleting Properties
Properties can be removed from an object using the delete operator.

Example:
```javascript
Copy code
delete car.year;
```
Checking for Properties

Use the in operator or hasOwnProperty() method to check if an object has a specific property.

in Operator:

javascript
Copy code
console.log('brand' in car); // Output: true

hasOwnProperty() Method:

javascript
Copy code
console.log(car.hasOwnProperty('model')); // Output: true

Object Methods

Methods are functions defined as properties of an object. They allow objects to perform actions or operations.

Defining Methods
Methods are defined like other properties but with function values.

Example:
javascript
Copy code
```
let person = {
  name: 'John',
  greet: function() {
    console.log('Hello, ' + this.name);
  }
};
```

person.greet(); // Output: Hello, John

Using the this Keyword

Inside a method, this refers to the object that owns the method. This allows methods to access other properties of the same object.

Example:
javascript
Copy code
```
let person = {
  name: 'Jane',
  age: 30,
  describe: function() {
```

```javascript
    return this.name + ' is ' + this.age + ' years old.';
  }
};
```

console.log(person.describe()); // Output: Jane is 30 years old.

Method Shorthand (ES6)

In ES6, you can use a shorthand syntax to define methods within an object.

Example:
javascript
Copy code
```javascript
let person = {
  name: 'John',
  greet() {
    console.log('Hello, ' + this.name);
  }
};
```

person.greet(); // Output: Hello, John
..

Summary

Working with object properties and methods involves creating, accessing, modifying, and deleting properties, as well as defining and using methods to perform actions related to the object. These operations are fundamental for managing and manipulating data within objects, allowing for organized and efficient code in JavaScript. Understanding these concepts helps in building complex structures and encapsulating data and functionality effectively.

Introduction to Arrays

In JavaScript, an array is a special type of object used to store ordered collections of data. Arrays are versatile data structures that allow you to manage and manipulate sequences of values efficiently. They are widely used for handling lists of items, such as numbers, strings, or objects.

Key Concepts
Definition:

An array is defined using square brackets [], with elements separated by commas. Arrays can hold values of any data type, including other arrays or objects.

Example:

```javascript
Copy code
let fruits = ['apple', 'banana', 'cherry'];
```

Indexing:
Array elements are accessed using numeric indices, starting from 0. Each element's position is determined by its index.

Example:

```javascript
Copy code
console.log(fruits[0]); // Output: apple
console.log(fruits[1]); // Output: banana
```

Length:
The length property of an array indicates the number of elements in the array.

Example:
javascript
Copy code
console.log(fruits.length); // Output: 3

Adding and Removing Elements:
Arrays provide methods for adding and removing elements.

Adding Elements:

push(): Adds elements to the end of an array.
javascript
Copy code
fruits.push('date');

unshift(): Adds elements to the beginning of an array.

javascript
Copy code
fruits.unshift('apricot');

Removing Elements:

pop(): Removes the last element of an array.
javascript

Copy code
```javascript
fruits.pop();
```

shift(): Removes the first element of an array.

javascript
Copy code
```javascript
fruits.shift();
```

Iterating Over Arrays:

Arrays can be traversed using loops and iteration methods.

For Loop:

javascript
Copy code
```javascript
for (let i = 0; i < fruits.length; i++) {
    console.log(fruits[i]);
}
```

forEach() Method:

javascript
Copy code

```javascript
fruits.forEach(function(fruit) {
    console.log(fruit);
});
```

Manipulating Arrays:

Arrays come with various built-in methods for manipulating and transforming data.

map(): Creates a new array with the results of calling a provided function on every element.

javascript
Copy code
```javascript
let lengths = fruits.map(fruit => fruit.length);
```
filter(): Creates a new array with all elements that pass the test implemented by the provided function.

javascript
Copy code
```javascript
let longFruits = fruits.filter(fruit => fruit.length > 5);
```
reduce(): Applies a function against an accumulator and each element to reduce it to a single value.

javascript

Copy code

```
let totalLength = fruits.reduce((acc, fruit) => acc +
fruit.length, 0);
```

Multidimensional Arrays:

Arrays can contain other arrays, creating multidimensional arrays.

Example:
javascript
Copy code

```javascript
let matrix = [
    [1, 2, 3],
    [4, 5, 6],
    [7, 8, 9]
];

console.log(matrix[1][2]); // Output: 6
```

Conclusion

Arrays are a powerful and flexible way to manage ordered collections of data in JavaScript. They provide various methods for accessing, modifying, and iterating over elements, making them essential for many programming tasks. Understanding how to work with arrays allows you to efficiently handle and manipulate data in your applications.

Common Array Methods

JavaScript arrays come with a wide range of built-in methods that facilitate common operations such as adding, removing, and transforming elements. Here are some of the most frequently used array methods:

1. push()
Purpose: Adds one or more elements to the end of an array.
Syntax: array.push(element1, element2, ..., elementN)

Example:
javascript
Copy code

```
let fruits = ['apple', 'banana'];
fruits.push('cherry');
```

console.log(fruits); // Output: ['apple', 'banana', 'cherry']

2. pop()
Purpose: Removes the last element from an array and returns it.
Syntax: array.pop()

Example:
javascript
Copy code
```javascript
let fruits = ['apple', 'banana', 'cherry'];
let lastFruit = fruits.pop();
console.log(lastFruit); // Output: 'cherry'
console.log(fruits); // Output: ['apple', 'banana']
```

3. shift()

Purpose: Removes the first element from an array and returns it.
Syntax: array.shift()
Example:
javascript
Copy code
```javascript
let fruits = ['apple', 'banana', 'cherry'];
let firstFruit = fruits.shift();
```

```javascript
console.log(firstFruit); // Output: 'apple'
console.log(fruits); // Output: ['banana', 'cherry']
```

4. unshift()

Purpose: Adds one or more elements to the beginning of an array.
Syntax: array.unshift(element1, element2, ..., elementN)
Example:
javascript
Copy code
```javascript
let fruits = ['banana', 'cherry'];
fruits.unshift('apple');
console.log(fruits); // Output: ['apple', 'banana', 'cherry']
```

5. splice()

Purpose: Adds or removes elements from a specific index in the array.
Syntax: array.splice(start, deleteCount, item1, item2, ..., itemN)
start: Index at which to start changes.
deleteCount: Number of elements to remove.
item1, item2, ..., itemN: Elements to add.

Example:
javascript
Copy code
```
let fruits = ['apple', 'banana', 'cherry'];
fruits.splice(1, 1, 'blueberry', 'date');
console.log(fruits); // Output: ['apple', 'blueberry', 'date', 'cherry']
```

6. slice()

Purpose: Creates a new array with a portion of the original array.
Syntax: array.slice(start, end)
start: Index to start the slice (inclusive).
end: Index to end the slice (exclusive).

Example:
javascript
Copy code
```
let fruits = ['apple', 'banana', 'cherry', 'date'];
let citrusFruits = fruits.slice(1, 3);
console.log(citrusFruits); // Output: ['banana', 'cherry']
```

7. forEach()

Purpose: Executes a provided function once for each array element.

Syntax: array.forEach(callback(element, index, array))

Example:
```javascript
Copy code
let fruits = ['apple', 'banana', 'cherry'];
fruits.forEach((fruit, index) => {
   console.log(index + ': ' + fruit);
});
```

8. map()

Purpose: Creates a new array with the results of calling a provided function on every element.

Syntax: array.map(callback(element, index, array))

Example:
```javascript
Copy code
let numbers = [1, 2, 3];
let squares = numbers.map(num => num * num);
console.log(squares); // Output: [1, 4, 9]
```

9. filter()

Purpose: Creates a new array with all elements that pass a test implemented by a provided function.
Syntax: array.filter(callback(element, index, array))

Example:

```javascript
Copy code
let numbers = [1, 2, 3, 4, 5];
let evenNumbers = numbers.filter(num => num % 2 === 0);
console.log(evenNumbers); // Output: [2, 4]
```

10. reduce()

Purpose: Applies a function against an accumulator and each element to reduce it to a single value.
Syntax: array.reduce(callback(accumulator, element, index, array), initialValue)
Example:

```javascript
Copy code
```

```javascript
let numbers = [1, 2, 3, 4];
let sum = numbers.reduce((acc, num) => acc + num, 0);
console.log(sum); // Output: 10
```

11. find()
Purpose: Returns the first element in the array that satisfies the provided testing function.
Syntax: array.find(callback(element, index, array))

Example:

javascript
Copy code
```javascript
let numbers = [4, 9, 16];
let firstEven = numbers.find(num => num % 2 === 0);
console.log(firstEven); // Output: 4
```

12. sort()
Purpose: Sorts the elements of an array in place and returns the sorted array.
Syntax: array.sort([compareFunction])

Example:
javascript
Copy code

```javascript
let numbers = [4, 1, 3, 2];
numbers.sort();
console.log(numbers); // Output: [1, 2, 3, 4]
```

13. reverse()

Purpose: Reverses the elements of an array in place.
Syntax: array.reverse()
Example:
javascript
Copy code
```javascript
let fruits = ['apple', 'banana', 'cherry'];
fruits.reverse();
console.log(fruits); // Output: ['cherry', 'banana', 'apple']
```

Conclusion

JavaScript arrays come equipped with a variety of methods to handle common tasks such as adding, removing, and transforming elements. Understanding and utilizing these methods effectively can help manage data collections and perform operations efficiently in your JavaScript applications.

Chapter 7
The Document Object Model (DOM)

The Document Object Model, commonly referred to as the DOM, is a programming interface for web documents. It represents the structure of a document as a tree of objects, allowing programs to interact with the content, structure, and style of web pages in a dynamic and programmable way.

Key Concepts
Document Structure:

The DOM represents an HTML or XML document as a tree structure, where each node corresponds to a part of the document. This includes elements, attributes, text, and other components.

For example, an HTML document might have the following structure:

html

Copy code

```
<!DOCTYPE html>
<html>
 <head>
  <title>Document Title</title>
 </head>
 <body>
  <h1>Main Heading</h1>
  <p>Paragraph of text.</p>
 </body>
</html>
```

In the DOM, this document would be represented as a tree of nodes with the html element at the root, containing head and body children, which in turn contain their respective child nodes.

Nodes and Elements:

The DOM is made up of nodes. The most common types of nodes are element nodes, attribute nodes, and text nodes.
Element Nodes: Represent HTML tags, like <body>, <h1>, and <p>.

Attribute Nodes: Represent attributes of HTML tags, such as class or id.

Text Nodes: Represent the text content within an element. DOM Manipulation:

JavaScript can be used to interact with the DOM, allowing you to create, remove, and modify elements and attributes. This enables dynamic content updates without the need to reload the page.

Selecting Elements: Methods like getElementById, getElementsByClassName, getElementsByTagName, querySelector, and querySelectorAll are used to select elements.

```javascript
Copy code
let heading = document.getElementById('main-heading');
let paragraphs = document.getElementsByClassName('text');
let firstParagraph = document.querySelector('p');
```

Changing Content and Attributes:

You can change the content and attributes of elements using various DOM properties and methods.

javascript
Copy code

```
let heading = document.getElementById('main-heading');
heading.textContent = 'New Heading'; // Changes the text content of the heading

let link = document.querySelector('a');
link.href = 'https://www.example.com'; // Changes the href attribute of the link
```

Creating and Removing Elements:

You can create new elements and add them to the document, as well as remove existing elements.

javascript
Copy code

```
// Creating a new element
let newParagraph = document.createElement('p');
newParagraph.textContent = 'This is a new paragraph.';
document.body.appendChild(newParagraph); // Adds the new paragraph to the body
```

```javascript
// Removing an element
let oldParagraph = document.getElementById('old-paragraph');
oldParagraph.remove();
```

Event Handling:

The DOM allows you to attach event listeners to elements, enabling you to respond to user interactions such as clicks, key presses, and mouse movements.
javascript
Copy code
```javascript
let button = document.getElementById('my-button');
button.addEventListener('click', function() {
    alert('Button was clicked!');
});
```

Conclusion

The DOM is a critical component of web development, providing a structured representation of a document and a way to interact with and manipulate it using JavaScript. Understanding the DOM and how to work with it is essential for creating dynamic and interactive web applications.

Understanding the DOM

The Document Object Model (DOM) is a powerful tool that allows developers to create dynamic and interactive web pages. Understanding the DOM is crucial for manipulating web content and enhancing user experiences.

What is the DOM?

The DOM is a programming interface for HTML and XML documents. It represents the document as a tree structure where each node is an object representing a part of the document, such as elements, attributes, or text. This tree-like representation enables scripts to update the content, structure, and style of a document dynamically.

DOM Structure

The DOM organizes a document into a hierarchical tree of nodes. There are different types of nodes, each serving a specific purpose:

Document Node: Represents the entire document.
Element Nodes: Represent HTML or XML elements (e.g., <body>, <div>, <p>).
Attribute Nodes: Represent the attributes of elements (e.g., class, id, src).
Text Nodes: Contain the text content within elements.
Comment Nodes: Represent comments in the document.

For example, the HTML snippet:

```
html
Copy code
<!DOCTYPE html>
<html>
 <head>
  <title>Document Title</title>
 </head>
 <body>
  <h1>Main Heading</h1>
  <p>Paragraph of text.</p>
 </body>
```

</html>

is represented in the DOM as a tree structure with nested nodes for the html, head, title, body, h1, and p elements, along with their respective text nodes.

Accessing DOM Elements
JavaScript provides various methods to access and manipulate DOM elements:

getElementById: Selects an element by its id attribute.

javascript
Copy code

```
let element = document.getElementById('example-id');
```

getElementsByClassName: Selects all elements with a specific class name.

javascript
Copy code

```
let elements = document.getElementsByClassName('example-class');
```

getElementsByTagName: Selects all elements with a specific tag name.

javascript
Copy code
```javascript
let elements = document.getElementsByTagName('p');
```
querySelector: Selects the first element that matches a CSS selector.

javascript
Copy code
```javascript
let element = document.querySelector('.example-class');
```
querySelectorAll: Selects all elements that match a CSS selector.

javascript
Copy code
```javascript
let elements = document.querySelectorAll('.example-class');
```
Manipulating DOM Elements

Once elements are selected, you can manipulate them in various ways:

Changing Content: Modify the text content of an element.

javascript
Copy code
```javascript
let heading = document.querySelector('h1');
heading.textContent = 'New Heading';
```

Changing Attributes: Modify the attributes of an element.

```javascript
Copy code
let link = document.querySelector('a');
link.href = 'https://www.example.com';
```

Adding Elements: Create new elements and add them to the DOM.

```javascript
Copy code
let newParagraph = document.createElement('p');
newParagraph.textContent = 'This is a new paragraph.';
document.body.appendChild(newParagraph);
```

Removing Elements: Remove elements from the DOM.

```javascript
Copy code
let                    oldParagraph                    =
document.getElementById('old-paragraph');
oldParagraph.remove();
```

Event Handling

The DOM allows you to attach event listeners to elements, enabling dynamic responses to user interactions:

Adding Event Listeners:

```javascript
Copy code
let button = document.getElementById('my-button');
button.addEventListener('click', function() {
    alert('Button was clicked!');
});
```

Removing Event Listeners:

```javascript
Copy code
let handler = function() {
    alert('Button was clicked!');
};
button.removeEventListener('click', handler);
```

Conclusion

Understanding the DOM is essential for web development as it provides the means to interact with and manipulate web documents dynamically. By mastering DOM access and manipulation techniques, you can create interactive, responsive, and engaging web applications.

Selecting and Manipulating DOM Elements

JavaScript's ability to interact with the Document Object Model (DOM) is fundamental to creating dynamic and interactive web pages. Selecting and manipulating DOM elements allows you to change the content, style, and structure of a web document in response to user actions or other events.

Selecting DOM Elements
To manipulate elements on a web page, you first need to select them. JavaScript provides several methods to do this, each with its own use cases:

getElementById:

Selects an element by its unique id attribute.

Example:
javascript
Copy code
let element = document.getElementById('header');
getElementsByClassName:

Selects all elements with a specific class name.
Returns an HTMLCollection (an array-like object).

Example:
javascript
Copy code
let elements = document.getElementsByClassName('menu-item');
getElementsByTagName:

Selects all elements with a specific tag name.

Returns an HTMLCollection.

Example:
javascript
Copy code
let elements = document.getElementsByTagName('p');

querySelector:

Selects the first element that matches a CSS selector.

Example:
javascript
Copy code
let element = document.querySelector('.menu-item');
querySelectorAll:

Selects all elements that match a CSS selector.

Returns a NodeList (another array-like object).

Example:
javascript
Copy code
let elements = document.querySelectorAll('.menu-item');

Manipulating DOM Elements

Once you've selected the elements, you can manipulate them in various ways to change their content, attributes, styles, and structure.

Changing Content

textContent:

Sets or returns the text content of an element.

Example:
javascript
Copy code
```
let heading = document.querySelector('h1');
heading.textContent = 'New Heading Text';
```
innerHTML:

Sets or returns the HTML content inside an element.

Example:
javascript
Copy code
```
let container = document.querySelector('.container');
container.innerHTML = '<p>New paragraph inside the container.</p>';
```

Changing Attributes

setAttribute:

Sets the value of an attribute on an element.
Example:
javascript
Copy code
let link = document.querySelector('a');
link.setAttribute('href', 'https://www.example.com');

getAttribute:

Returns the value of an attribute on an element.

Example:
javascript
Copy code
let link = document.querySelector('a');
let href = link.getAttribute('href');

removeAttribute:

Removes an attribute from an element.
Example:
javascript
Copy code
let image = document.querySelector('img');
image.removeAttribute('alt');

Changing Styles
Directly Setting style Property:

Example:
javascript
Copy code

```javascript
let element = document.querySelector('.highlight');
element.style.backgroundColor = 'yellow';
```

Adding or Removing CSS Classes:

Using classList.add and classList.remove.
Example:
javascript
Copy code

```javascript
let element = document.querySelector('.menu-item');
element.classList.add('active');
element.classList.remove('inactive');
```

Adding and Removing Elements

Creating New Elements:

Example:
javascript

Copy code

```
let newParagraph = document.createElement('p');
newParagraph.textContent = 'This is a new paragraph.';
document.body.appendChild(newParagraph);
```

Removing Elements:

Example:
javascript
Copy code

```
let oldParagraph = document.querySelector('.old-paragraph');
oldParagraph.remove();
```

Inserting Elements:

appendChild: Adds a new child element to the end of a parent element.

javascript
Copy code

```
let list = document.querySelector('ul');
let newItem = document.createElement('li');
newItem.textContent = 'New Item';
list.appendChild(newItem);
```

insertBefore: Inserts a new element before an existing child element.

javascript
Copy code
```
let list = document.querySelector('ul');
let newItem = document.createElement('li');
newItem.textContent = 'New Item';
let firstItem = list.firstElementChild;
list.insertB
efore(newItem, firstItem);
```

Event Handling

Attaching event listeners to DOM elements allows you to execute JavaScript code in response to user actions such as clicks, mouse movements, or keyboard inputs.

addEventListener:

Example:
javascript
Copy code
```
let button = document.querySelector('button');
button.addEventListener('click', function() {
```

```javascript
  alert('Button clicked!');
});
removeEventListener:
```

Example:

```javascript
javascript
Copy code
let button = document.querySelector('button');
let handleClick = function() {
    alert('Button clicked!');
};
button.addEventListener('click', handleClick);
button.removeEventListener('click', handleClick);
```

Conclusion

Selecting and manipulating DOM elements is a fundamental skill for web developers. By understanding how to access and modify elements, attributes, and styles, you can create dynamic and responsive web applications that respond to user interactions and provide a richer user experience.

Event Handling

Event handling is a core concept in web development that enables developers to make web pages interactive. By responding to user actions like clicks, key presses, and mouse movements, you can create dynamic and engaging user experiences.

Understanding Events
An event is a signal that something has happened in the web page. Examples of common events include:

Mouse Events: click, dblclick, mousedown, mouseup, mousemove, mouseover, mouseout.

Keyboard Events: keydown, keyup, keypress.
Form Events: submit, focus, blur, change, input.
Window Events: load, resize, scroll.

Adding Event Listeners
Event listeners are functions that execute in response to an event. You can attach event listeners to HTML elements

using JavaScript, allowing your code to respond to user interactions.

Using addEventListener

The addEventListener method is the most versatile way to add event listeners. It allows you to attach multiple listeners to a single element and provides options for controlling event propagation.

javascript
Copy code

```javascript
let button = document.getElementById('my-button');
button.addEventListener('click', function() {
    alert('Button was clicked!');
});
```

.

Removing Event Listeners

If you need to remove an event listener, use the removeEventListener method. This requires a reference to the function used as the event handler.

javascript
Copy code

```javascript
let button = document.getElementById('my-button');
function handleClick() {
    alert('Button was clicked!');
}
button.addEventListener('click', handleClick);
// Later, remove the event listener
button.removeEventListener('click', handleClick);
```

Event Object

When an event occurs, an event object is created containing information about the event. This object is passed to the event handler function, providing access to details such as the event type, target element, and coordinates.

javascript
Copy code
```javascript
let button = document.getElementById('my-button');
button.addEventListener('click', function(event) {
    console.log('Event type:', event.type);
    console.log('Target element:', event.target);
});
```

Event Propagation

Event propagation describes how events travel through the DOM tree. There are three phases:

Capturing Phase: The event travels down from the root to the target element.

Target Phase: The event reaches the target element.
Bubbling Phase: The event bubbles up from the target element to the root.

By default, event listeners respond during the bubbling phase. You can specify the capturing phase by setting the useCapture parameter to true in addEventListener.

javascript
Copy code
```
let container = document.getElementById('container');
let button = document.getElementById('my-button');

container.addEventListener('click', function() {
    console.log('Container clicked');
}, true);

button.addEventListener('click', function() {
    console.log('Button clicked');
```

```
});
```

Preventing Default Behavior

Some events have default behaviors (e.g., submitting a form, clicking a link). You can prevent these behaviors using the preventDefault method on the event object.

```javascript
Copy code
let link = document.getElementById('my-link');
link.addEventListener('click', function(event) {
    event.preventDefault();
    console.log('Default behavior prevented');
});
```

Event Delegation

Event delegation is a technique where a single event listener is added to a parent element to manage events for multiple child elements. This is efficient for dynamically created elements and reduces the number of event listeners.

javascript

Copy code

```
let list = document.getElementById('my-list');
list.addEventListener('click', function(event) {
  if (event.target.tagName === 'LI') {
                        console.log('List    item    clicked:',
event.target.textContent);
  }
});
```

Conclusion

Event handling is essential for creating interactive web applications. By understanding how to add, remove, and manage event listeners, you can respond to user actions effectively and create dynamic, responsive web pages. Leveraging techniques like event delegation and understanding event propagation will help you write more efficient and maintainable code.

Chapter 8
Advanced JavaScript Concepts

As you advance in your JavaScript journey, understanding more complex and nuanced concepts becomes crucial. These advanced topics enable you to write more efficient, robust, and maintainable code, and help you harness the full power of JavaScript. In this section, we will explore some key advanced JavaScript concepts, including closures, asynchronous programming, the event loop, prototypal inheritance, and modules.

Closures allow functions to access variables from an enclosing scope, even after that scope has exited, enabling powerful programming patterns. Asynchronous programming, through callbacks, promises, and async/await, allows JavaScript to handle operations like network requests without blocking the execution of other code. The event loop, a core part of JavaScript's concurrency model, manages how JavaScript handles asynchronous operations, ensuring that the execution of code remains non-blocking and efficient.

Prototypal inheritance is a fundamental concept that underlies how objects and methods are shared in JavaScript, promoting code reuse and flexibility. Modules, introduced in ES6, allow for the organization of code into reusable, maintainable pieces, making complex applications easier to manage and develop.

By mastering these advanced concepts, you'll be well-equipped to tackle complex JavaScript applications and create high-performance, scalable solutions.

Understanding the 'this' Keyword

The ' this' keyword in JavaScript is a fundamental yet often misunderstood concept. It is used to reference the context in which a function is executed, providing a way to access properties and methods within that context. The value of this changes depending on how a function is called, making it both powerful and sometimes confusing.

Different Contexts of this

Global Context

In the global execution context (outside of any function), this refers to the global object. In a browser, this is the window object.

```javascript
Copy code
console.log(this); // window
```

Function Context

When a function is called as a standalone function, this refers to the global object (in non-strict mode) or undefined (in strict mode).

```javascript
Copy code
function showThis() {
    console.log(this);
}
showThis(); // window (or undefined in strict mode)
```

Method Context

When a function is called as a method of an object, this refers to the object the method is called on.

javascript
Copy code
```javascript
let obj = {
  name: 'Alice',
  greet: function() {
    console.log(this.name);
  }
};
obj.greet(); // Alice
```

Constructor Context

When a function is used as a constructor with the new keyword, this refers to the newly created instance of the object.

javascript
Copy code
```javascript
function Person(name) {
  this.name = name;
}
```

```javascript
let person1 = new Person('Alice');
console.log(person1.name); // Alice
```

Arrow Functions

Arrow functions do not have their own this context. Instead, they inherit this from the enclosing lexical context (the context in which they were defined).

```javascript
Copy code
let obj = {
  name: 'Alice',
  greet: function() {
    let innerGreet = () => {
      console.log(this.name);
    };
    innerGreet();
  }
};
obj.greet(); // Alice
```

Binding this

In some cases, you may need to explicitly set the value of this to ensure it points to the correct context. JavaScript provides several methods to achieve this:

call and apply Methods
These methods allow you to call a function with a specified this value and arguments.

javascript
Copy code
```
function greet(greeting) {
    console.log(greeting + ', ' + this.name);
}
let person = { name: 'Alice' };
greet.call(person, 'Hello'); // Hello, Alice
greet.apply(person, ['Hi']); // Hi, Alice
```

bind Method

The bind method creates a new function that, when called, has its this value set to the specified value.

javascript
Copy code
```
let person = { name: 'Alice' };
```

```javascript
let greetBound = greet.bind(person);
greetBound('Hello'); // Hello, Alice
```

Common Pitfalls

Understanding the this keyword can be tricky due to its dynamic nature. Here are some common pitfalls:

Losing this in Callbacks
When passing a method as a callback, this can be lost.

javascript
Copy code
```javascript
let obj = {
  name: 'Alice',
  greet: function() {
    console.log(this.name);
  }
};
setTimeout(obj.greet, 1000); // undefined (or error in strict mode)
```

To fix this, you can use bind, an arrow function, or a variable to capture this.

javascript

```
setTimeout(obj.greet.bind(obj), 1000); // Alice
setTimeout(() => obj.greet(), 1000); // Alice

let self = obj;
setTimeout(function() {
  self.greet();
}, 1000); // Alice
```

Event Handlers

In event handlers, this refers to the element that received the event.

javascript

```
document.getElementById('myButton').addEventListener('click', function() {
  console.log(this.id); // myButton
});
```

To use the correct context within an event handler, you might use bind or an arrow function.

javascript

```javascript
let obj = {
  name: 'Alice',
  greet: function() {
    console.log(this.name);
  }
};
document.getElementById('myButton').addEventListener('click', obj.greet.bind(obj)); // Alice

document.getElementById('myButton').addEventListener('click', () => obj.greet()); // Alice
```

Conclusion

The this keyword is a crucial part of JavaScript that enables functions to have dynamic context. Understanding how this behaves in different scenarios, and how to control its value using call, apply, and bind, is essential for writing robust and maintainable code. By mastering this, you can avoid common pitfalls and leverage its power to create more dynamic and flexible applications.

Prototypes and Inheritance

In JavaScript, prototypes are a fundamental concept for creating and managing object inheritance. The prototype-based inheritance system enables objects to share properties and methods through a chain of prototypes, allowing for the reuse of code and the extension of functionality.

Prototypes

Every JavaScript object has a prototype object, which can be accessed through the internal [[Prototype]] property. This prototype object itself can have its own prototype, forming a prototype chain. When you access a property or method on an object, JavaScript first looks on the object itself and then follows the prototype chain until it finds the property or reaches the end of the chain.

Prototype Chain

The prototype chain is a series of links between objects, allowing properties and methods to be inherited. If a property is not found on an object, JavaScript checks the object's prototype, and then the prototype's prototype, and so on.

Creating Prototypes

Constructor Functions

Constructor functions are used to create objects and define methods that are shared across all instances. The methods are added to the constructor's prototype property.

```javascript
Copy code
function Animal(name) {
    this.name = name;
}

Animal.prototype.speak = function() {
    console.log(this.name + ' makes a noise.');
};

let animal1 = new Animal('Generic Animal');
animal1.speak(); // Generic Animal makes a noise.
```

Object.create Method

The Object.create method creates a new object with a specified prototype object. This is useful for setting up inheritance directly.

```javascript
Copy code
let animalPrototype = {
  speak: function() {
    console.log(this.name + ' makes a noise.');
  }
};

let dog = Object.create(animalPrototype);
dog.name = 'Rex';
dog.speak(); // Rex makes a noise.
```

Inheritance

JavaScript supports prototype-based inheritance, allowing one object to inherit properties and methods from another. This is often implemented using constructor functions or ES6 classes.

Constructor Function Inheritance

To set up inheritance using constructor functions, you assign the prototype of the child constructor to a new object created from the parent constructor's prototype.

```javascript
Copy code
function Animal(name) {
  this.name = name;
}

Animal.prototype.speak = function() {
  console.log(this.name + ' makes a noise.');
};

function Dog(name, breed) {
  Animal.call(this, name);
  this.breed = breed;
}

// Set up inheritance
Dog.prototype = Object.create(Animal.prototype);
Dog.prototype.constructor = Dog;

Dog.prototype.speak = function() {
  console.log(this.name + ' barks.');
```

```javascript
};

let dog1 = new Dog('Rex', 'Golden Retriever');
dog1.speak(); // Rex barks.
```

ES6 Classes

ES6 introduced class syntax, providing a more straightforward way to set up inheritance while still using prototypes under the hood.

javascript
Copy code
```javascript
class Animal {
  constructor(name) {
    this.name = name;
  }

  speak() {
    console.log(this.name + ' makes a noise.');
  }
}

class Dog extends Animal {
```

```
  constructor(name, breed) {
    super(name);
    this.breed = breed;
  }

  speak() {
    console.log(this.name + ' barks.');
  }
}

let dog1 = new Dog('Rex', 'Golden Retriever');
dog1.speak(); // Rex barks.
```

Prototype Properties and Methods

Object.getPrototypeOf: Returns the prototype of a given object.
Object.setPrototypeOf: Sets the prototype of a given object.
Object.hasOwnProperty: Checks if a property is directly on the object, not inherited through the prototype chain.

Conclusion

Prototypes and inheritance are key concepts in JavaScript that enable the creation of flexible and reusable code. By understanding how prototypes work and how to use them for inheritance, you can build more efficient and maintainable applications. Whether using constructor functions or ES6 classes, these mechanisms help you leverage object-oriented principles in JavaScript.

Asynchronous JavaScript (Promises, async/await)

Asynchronous JavaScript is essential for handling operations that do not complete immediately, such as network requests, file reading, or timers. Promises and the async/await syntax provide powerful tools for managing asynchronous operations, making code easier to write and understand.

Promises

Promises represent the eventual completion (or failure) of an asynchronous operation and its resulting value. They provide a cleaner way to handle asynchronous operations compared to traditional callback-based approaches.

Creating a Promise

A Promise is created using the Promise constructor, which takes a function with two arguments: resolve and reject. These arguments are functions used to settle the promise.

```javascript
Copy code
let promise = new Promise((resolve, reject) => {
    let success = true; // Simulate success or failure
    if (success) {
        resolve('Operation was successful');
    } else {
        reject('Operation failed');
    }
});
```

Using Promises

Promises have three states:

Pending: The initial state, neither fulfilled nor rejected.
Fulfilled: The operation completed successfully.
Rejected: The operation failed.

You use .then() to handle fulfillment and .catch() to handle rejection.

javascript
Copy code

```javascript
promise
  .then((result) => {
    console.log(result); // Operation was successful
  })
  .catch((error) => {
    console.error(error); // Operation failed
  });
```

You can chain multiple .then() calls to handle sequential asynchronous operations.

javascript
Copy code

```javascript
promise
  .then((result) => {
    console.log(result);
    return 'Another operation';
  })
  .then((message) => {
    console.log(message); // Another operation
```

```
})
.catch((error) => {
  console.error(error);
});
```

async/await

The async/await syntax, introduced in ES2017, provides a more readable and concise way to handle asynchronous code. It simplifies working with promises by allowing you to write asynchronous code that looks and behaves like synchronous code.

Defining Async Functions

An async function always returns a promise. Inside an async function, you use the await keyword to pause the execution until the promise is resolved or rejected.

```javascript
Copy code
async function fetchData() {
  return 'Data fetched';
}
```

```javascript
fetchData().then(result => {
    console.log(result); // Data fetched
});
```

Using await

The await keyword is used inside async functions to wait for a promise to resolve. It effectively pauses the execution of the function until the promise is resolved.

javascript
Copy code
```javascript
async function getData() {
    let data = await fetch('https://api.example.com/data');
    let json = await data.json();
    console.log(json);
}
```

Error Handling

You handle errors in async/await functions using try...catch blocks, which provides a more familiar way to manage exceptions.

javascript

```
Copy code
async function getData() {
  try {
                                let response = await
fetch('https://api.example.com/data');
    let json = await response.json();
    console.log(json);
  } catch (error) {
    console.error('Error:', error);
  }
}
```

Combining Promises and async/await

You can use async/await with existing promise-based APIs, providing a more readable way to handle asynchronous operations.

javascript
Copy code
```
async function processData() {
  try {
    let result = await new Promise((resolve, reject) => {
      setTimeout(() => resolve('Processed data'), 1000);
    });
```

```
    console.log(result); // Processed data
  } catch (error) {
    console.error('Error:', error);
  }
}
```

Conclusion

Asynchronous JavaScript is crucial for handling operations that may take time to complete. Promises provide a way to manage asynchronous code with cleaner syntax compared to callbacks, while async/await further simplifies asynchronous programming, making it easier to read and maintain. By mastering these concepts, you can effectively manage asynchronous operations and write more efficient and reliable JavaScript code.

Chapter 9
JavaScript in the Browser

JavaScript is a fundamental technology for creating dynamic and interactive web applications. In the browser environment, JavaScript enhances the user experience by allowing developers to manipulate HTML and CSS, respond to user events, and communicate with servers. Understanding how JavaScript operates within the browser is essential for building modern, responsive websites.

Key Aspects of JavaScript in the Browser
Manipulating the DOM: JavaScript interacts with the Document Object Model (DOM), which represents the

structure of the web page. By modifying the DOM, you can change the content, structure, and style of a web page dynamically in response to user actions or other events.

Handling Events: JavaScript allows you to handle various user events, such as clicks, key presses, and mouse movements. By attaching event listeners to HTML elements, you can create interactive features and respond to user input in real time.

Asynchronous Communication: JavaScript can make asynchronous requests to servers using technologies like XMLHttpRequest and the Fetch API. This enables you to update web content without requiring a full page reload, enhancing the user experience with faster and more seamless interactions.

Browser APIs: JavaScript provides access to a range of browser-specific APIs that enable features like local storage, geolocation, and multimedia handling. These APIs extend the capabilities of your web applications and allow for richer interactions with users.

By understanding these core aspects, you can leverage JavaScript to build engaging and responsive web applications that provide a better user experience and meet modern web standards.

Browser Events and Event Listeners

Browser events are actions or occurrences that happen in the browser, such as user interactions, changes in state, or other significant occurrences. JavaScript provides a way to respond to these events through event listeners, enabling you to create interactive and dynamic web applications.

Types of Browser Events

User Interaction Events

Click: Triggered when an element is clicked.
Double-click: Triggered when an element is double-clicked.
Mouseover / Mouseout: Triggered when the mouse pointer enters or leaves an element.
Keydown / Keyup: Triggered when a key is pressed or released.
Form Events

Submit: Triggered when a form is submitted.

Change: Triggered when the value of a form element changes.

Input: Triggered when the value of an input element changes, including while typing.

Window Events

Load: Triggered when the entire page and its resources are fully loaded.

Resize: Triggered when the browser window is resized.

Scroll: Triggered when the user scrolls the page.

Focus Events

Focus: Triggered when an element gains focus.

Blur: Triggered when an element loses focus.

Event Listeners

Event listeners are functions that respond to specific events on an element. You can attach event listeners to HTML elements using JavaScript, specifying the type of event to listen for and the function to execute when the event occurs.

Adding Event Listeners

Use the addEventListener method to attach an event listener to an element:

```javascript
Copy code
document.getElementById('myButton').addEventListener('click', function() {
    alert('Button clicked!');
});
```

In this example, an alert is displayed when the button with the ID myButton is clicked.

Removing Event Listeners

You can remove an event listener using the removeEventListener method. To do this, you need to pass the exact function reference that was used with addEventListener.

```javascript
Copy code
function handleClick() {
    alert('Button clicked!');
}
```

```javascript
let button = document.getElementById('myButton');
button.addEventListener('click', handleClick);

// Later, to remove the event listener
button.removeEventListener('click', handleClick);
```

Event Object

When an event occurs, an event object is automatically passed to the event handler function. This object contains information about the event, such as the type of event, the target element, and additional properties relevant to the event.

javascript
Copy code
```javascript
document.getElementById('myButton').addEventListener('click', function(event) {
    console.log(event.type); // 'click'
    console.log(event.target); // The element that was clicked
});
```

Event Delegation

Event delegation is a technique where a single event listener is attached to a parent element, rather than multiple listeners on individual child elements. This approach is useful for dynamically added elements and can improve performance by reducing the number of event listeners.

```javascript
Copy code
document.getElementById('parentElement').addEventListener('click', function(event) {
                if (event.target &&
event.target.matches('button.childElement')) {
    alert('Child button clicked!');
  }
});
```

In this example, the click event on the parent element is used to handle clicks on child buttons.

Conclusion
Browser events and event listeners are fundamental to creating interactive web applications. By understanding how to work with different types of events and how to use event listeners effectively, you can build responsive and engaging

user interfaces that react dynamically to user interactions and other changes in the browser environment.

.

Forms and User Input

Forms are a key element of web development, allowing users to submit data and interact with web applications. JavaScript enhances forms by providing methods for validation, dynamic updates, and improved user experiences. Understanding how to manage and manipulate forms and user input is crucial for creating functional and interactive web applications.

Basic Form Elements
Input Fields: Collect various types of data from users, including text, numbers, and dates. Common input types include <input type="text">, <input type="email">, <input type="number">, and <input type="password">.

Text Areas: Allow for multi-line text input. Implemented with the <textarea> tag.

Select Menus: Provide a dropdown list of options for users to choose from. Created using the <select> tag with <option> elements.

Checkboxes and Radio Buttons: Allow users to select one or more options from a set. Checkboxes are created with <input type="checkbox">, and radio buttons with <input type="radio">.

Buttons: Trigger form submissions or other actions. Implemented with the <button> or <input type="button"> tag.

Handling Form Submission
JavaScript provides ways to handle form submissions and interact with form data:

Accessing Form Elements
You can access form elements using methods such as getElementById, querySelector, or elements property of the form.

javascript
Copy code
```javascript
let form = document.getElementById('myForm');
let input = form.elements['username'].value;
```

Form Submission Event

To handle form submission, you can listen for the submit event. This allows you to validate or modify the form data before it is sent to the server.

javascript
Copy code
```javascript
document.getElementById('myForm').addEventListener('submit', function(event) {
    event.preventDefault(); // Prevents the default form submission

    let username = document.getElementById('username').value;
    console.log('Form submitted with username:', username);
});
```

Form Validation
JavaScript can be used to validate form inputs before submission, ensuring that the data meets specific criteria.

Basic Validation

You can check values directly within the submit event handler or use HTML5 validation attributes such as required, minlength, and pattern.

```javascript
Copy code
document.getElementById('myForm').addEventListener('submit', function(event) {
    let username = document.getElementById('username').value;
  if (username.trim() === '') {
    alert('Username is required');
    event.preventDefault(); // Prevents form submission
  }
});
```

HTML5 Validation

HTML5 introduces built-in validation features. For example, setting the required attribute on an input field ensures that the field must be filled out before the form can be submitted.

html
Copy code

```html
<input type="text" id="username" required>
```

Handling User Input

JavaScript can dynamically interact with user input, updating the UI or performing calculations as the user types or selects options.

Listening to Input Events

Use events like input, change, and focus to respond to user input in real time.

javascript
Copy code

```javascript
document.getElementById('username').addEventListener('input', function(event) {
    let value = event.target.value;
    console.log('Username input:', value);
});
```

Updating the UI

JavaScript can dynamically update the content or style of the page based on user input.

javascript
Copy code

```
document.getElementById('username').addEventListener('input', function(event) {

document.getElementById('displayUsername').textContent = event.target.value;
});
```

.Sending Form Data

JavaScript can be used to send form data asynchronously without reloading the page using the Fetch API or XMLHttpRequest.

javascript
Copy code

```
document.getElementById('myForm').addEventListener('submit', function(event) {
    event.preventDefault();
    let formData = new FormData(this);
```

```
fetch('/submit', {
  method: 'POST',
  body: formData
})
.then(response => response.json())
.then(data => {
  console.log('Success:', data);
})
.catch(error => {
  console.error('Error:', error);
});
});
```

Conclusion

Forms and user input are central to web interactions, allowing users to provide data and engage with applications. By leveraging JavaScript, you can enhance forms with dynamic behavior, validate input, and handle submissions efficiently. Understanding how to manipulate forms and manage user input effectively is essential for creating interactive and user-friendly web experiences.

Validating Form Data

Validating form data is a crucial step in ensuring that user inputs are accurate, complete, and secure before they are processed or sent to a server. Effective validation helps prevent errors, improve user experience, and safeguard against malicious inputs.

Types of Validation

Client-Side Validation

Client-side validation occurs in the user's browser before the form data is submitted to the server. It provides immediate feedback to users and reduces the number of invalid submissions.

Server-Side Validation

Server-side validation takes place after the form data is submitted and received by the server. It is essential for security and data integrity, as client-side validation can be bypassed or manipulated.

Client-Side Validation Techniques

HTML5 Validation Attributes
HTML5 provides built-in attributes for basic validation, including:

required: Ensures that the input field is not empty.

html
Copy code
```
<input type="text" id="username" required>
```
minlength / maxlength: Sets minimum and maximum length constraints for text fields.

html
Copy code
```
<input type="text" id="username" minlength="3" maxlength="15" required>
```
pattern: Defines a regular expression that the input must match.

html
Copy code

```
<input          type="text"          id="email"
pattern="[a-z0-9._%+-]+@[a-z0-9.-]+\.[a-z]{2,}$" required>
```
type: Specifies the type of data expected, such as email, number, url, etc.

html
Copy code
```
<input type="email" id="email" required>
```

JavaScript Validation

JavaScript allows for more complex and dynamic validation. You can use event listeners to check form data before submission or as the user interacts with the form.

javascript
Copy code
```
document.getElementById('myForm').addEventListener('submit', function(event) {
    let username = document.getElementById('username').value;
    let email = document.getElementById('email').value;

    if (username.length < 3) {
        alert('Username must be at least 3 characters long.');
```

```javascript
    event.preventDefault(); // Prevent form submission
  }

  let emailPattern = /^[^\s@]+@[^\s@]+\.[^\s@]+$/;
  if (!emailPattern.test(email)) {
    alert('Please enter a valid email address.');
    event.preventDefault(); // Prevent form submission
  }
});
```

Dynamic Validation

You can provide real-time feedback to users as they enter data using event listeners on input fields.

javascript
Copy code
```javascript
document.getElementById('username').addEventListener('input', function() {
  let value = this.value;
  if (value.length < 3) {
        this.setCustomValidity('Username must be at least 3 characters long.');
  } else {
    this.setCustomValidity('');
```

```
  }
});
```

Server-Side Validation

While client-side validation enhances user experience, server-side validation is essential for security and data integrity. This validation occurs on the server after the form is submitted.

Validation Libraries

Many server-side languages and frameworks provide validation libraries or functions. For example, in Node.js, you can use libraries like validator or express-validator.

```javascript
Copy code
const { check, validationResult } = require('express-validator');

app.post('/submit', [
  check('username').isLength({ min: 3 }),
  check('email').isEmail()
], (req, res) => {
```

```javascript
  const errors = validationResult(req);
  if (!errors.isEmpty()) {
    return res.status(400).json({ errors: errors.array() });
  }
  // Process valid data
});
```

Custom Validation

You can implement custom validation logic based on your specific requirements. This often includes checking for unique values, ensuring data consistency, and more.

javascript
Copy code
```javascript
app.post('/submit', (req, res) => {
  let username = req.body.username;
  let email = req.body.email;

  if (username.length < 3) {
    return res.status(400).send('Username must be at least 3 characters long.');
  }

  if (!validateEmail(email)) {
```

```
    return res.status(400).send('Invalid email address.');
  }

  // Process valid data
});

function validateEmail(email) {
  let emailPattern = /^[^\s@]+@[^\s@]+\.[^\s@]+$/;
  return emailPattern.test(email);
}
```

Conclusion

Validating form data is crucial for ensuring data accuracy, improving user experience, and maintaining security. By combining client-side and server-side validation techniques, you can effectively handle user input, provide immediate feedback, and safeguard against invalid or malicious data.

Chapter 10
Working with APIs

APIs (Application Programming Interfaces) are vital tools that allow different software systems to interact and exchange data. They provide standardized ways for applications to request and receive information, enabling integration with external services, databases, and platforms. Mastering API interactions involves understanding how to make requests, handle responses, and manage authentication, which can significantly enhance the functionality and connectivity of your applications.

Introduction to APIs

APIs, or Application Programming Interfaces, are essential components in modern software development. They define a set of rules and protocols for building and interacting with software applications, allowing different systems to communicate and share data seamlessly. APIs are like bridges that connect disparate systems, enabling them to work together and extend their functionalities.

Key Concepts

What is an API?

An API is a set of defined interactions between different software components. It specifies how requests should be made and what responses will be returned. APIs allow developers to integrate external services, access data, and perform complex operations without needing to understand the internal workings of the systems they interact with.

Types of APIs

Web APIs: Accessible over the internet, often using HTTP/HTTPS protocols. Common examples include RESTful APIs, GraphQL APIs, and SOAP APIs.
Library APIs: Provided by software libraries or frameworks to expose their functionalities to other software.
Operating System APIs: Allow applications to interact with the underlying operating system, such as file management or network operations.

Endpoints

An API endpoint is a specific URL where API requests are directed. Each endpoint corresponds to a particular resource or action, such as retrieving user data or submitting a form.

Requests and Responses

Request: An API call made by the client, which includes an HTTP method (GET, POST, PUT, DELETE), a URL (endpoint), headers, and a body (optional).
Response: The data returned by the server, typically in JSON or XML format, including status codes to indicate the success or failure of the request.
Authentication
Many APIs require authentication to ensure secure access. Common methods include API keys, OAuth tokens, and JWT (JSON Web Tokens). Authentication verifies the identity of the client making the request and controls access to the API.

How APIs Work

Client Makes a Request: The client application sends an HTTP request to a specific API endpoint with the necessary parameters and authentication details.

Server Processes the Request: The server receives the request, processes it according to its rules, and interacts with any underlying systems or databases as needed.

Server Sends a Response: The server sends back a response to the client, containing the requested data or the result of the operation.

Client Processes the Response: The client application receives the response and processes it, updating the user interface or performing further actions based on the data received.

Why Use APIs?

Integration: APIs allow applications to integrate with other services and platforms, expanding their capabilities without reinventing the wheel.

Data Access: APIs provide access to remote data and functionalities, enabling applications to retrieve and use information from various sources.

Modularity: APIs enable modular design, allowing different components of a system to interact and function independently while working together.

Efficiency: By using APIs, developers can leverage existing solutions and services, saving time and resources in building complex functionalities.

Conclusion

APIs are fundamental to modern software development, enabling seamless integration, data exchange, and extended functionalities. Understanding how APIs work and how to interact with them is crucial for building dynamic and interconnected applications that leverage external services and data sources.

Fetching Data from APIs

Fetching data from APIs is a common task in web development, allowing applications to retrieve and utilize information from external sources. This process involves sending requests to API endpoints and handling the responses to integrate the data into your application.

Key Concepts

Making API Requests
To fetch data, you need to make an HTTP request to the API's endpoint. The request typically includes:

HTTP Method: Common methods include GET (to retrieve data), POST (to submit data), PUT (to update data), and DELETE (to remove data).

URL (Endpoint): The specific address where the API is accessed.

Headers: Additional information such as authentication tokens or content type.

Body: Data sent with the request, used mainly with POST and PUT requests.

Handling Responses

The API responds with data, usually in JSON or XML format. The response includes:

Status Code: Indicates the result of the request (e.g., 200 for success, 404 for not found, 500 for server error).
Response Body: Contains the requested data or error message.

Headers: Additional metadata about the response.

Fetching Data with JavaScript
JavaScript provides various methods to fetch data from APIs, with the Fetch API being the most modern and widely used approach.

Using Fetch API
The Fetch API provides a simple, promise-based method to make HTTP requests and handle responses.

javascript
Copy code
```
fetch('https://api.example.com/data')
```

```javascript
.then(response => {
  if (!response.ok) {
    throw new Error('Network response was not ok');
  }
  return response.json(); // Parse JSON data
})
.then(data => {
  console.log(data); // Process the data
})
.catch(error => {
    console.error('There was a problem with the fetch operation:', error);
  });
```

.then(): Handles successful responses.

.catch(): Catches and handles errors.

Using XMLHttpRequest

Although Fetch API is preferred, XMLHttpRequest is still used in some legacy codebases.

javascript
Copy code
```javascript
let xhr = new XMLHttpRequest();
xhr.open('GET', 'https://api.example.com/data', true);
```

```javascript
xhr.onload = function() {
    if (xhr.status >= 200 && xhr.status < 300) {
        let data = JSON.parse(xhr.responseText);
        console.log(data); // Process the data
    } else {
        console.error('Request failed');
    }
};
xhr.onerror = function() {
    console.error('Request error');
};
xhr.send();
```

xhr.onload: Handles successful responses.

xhr.onerror: Handles network errors.

Handling Authentication

If the API requires authentication, include necessary credentials in the request headers.

javascript
Copy code
```javascript
fetch('https://api.example.com/secure-data', {
    headers: {
        'Authorization': 'Bearer YOUR_ACCESS_TOKEN'
```

```javascript
  }
})
.then(response => response.json())
.then(data => console.log(data))
.catch(error => console.error('Error:', error));
```

Error Handling

Handling errors gracefully is crucial for a robust application. Common types of errors include network issues, invalid responses, and authentication failures. Implement proper error handling to manage these scenarios effectively.

javascript
Copy code
```javascript
fetch('https://api.example.com/data')
  .then(response => {
    if (!response.ok) {
      throw new Error('Network response was not ok');
    }
    return response.json();
  })
  .then(data => console.log(data))
```

```
.catch(error => console.error('There was a problem with
your fetch operation:', error));
```

Conclusion

Fetching data from APIs is a fundamental part of modern web development, enabling applications to access and use external information. By using methods like Fetch API or XMLHttpRequest, handling responses and errors, and managing authentication, developers can effectively integrate API data into their applications, enhancing functionality and user experience.

Handling API Responses

Handling API responses is a critical step in integrating external services into your application. Once your application sends a request to an API, it receives a response that must be processed and utilized effectively. Proper handling of API responses ensures that the data is correctly interpreted, errors are managed, and the application remains robust and user-friendly.

Key Concepts

Understanding Response Structure
API responses typically consist of:

Status Code: Indicates the result of the request. Common status codes include:
200 OK: Request succeeded.
201 Created: Resource successfully created.
204 No Content: Request succeeded but no data returned.
400 Bad Request: Client-side error, often due to invalid input.
401 Unauthorized: Authentication required or failed.
404 Not Found: Requested resource does not exist.
500 Internal Server Error: Server-side issue.

Response Body: Contains the data or error message, often in JSON format.

Headers: Additional metadata about the response, such as content type or rate limit information.

Parsing the Response

The response body is typically in JSON format, which needs to be parsed into a JavaScript object for further processing.

javascript
Copy code
```javascript
fetch('https://api.example.com/data')
  .then(response => response.json()) // Parse JSON data
  .then(data => {
    console.log(data); // Use the parsed data
  });
```

Handling Successful Responses

Once the response is parsed, you can process the data as needed. This may involve updating the user interface, performing calculations, or storing the data.

javascript
Copy code
```javascript
fetch('https://api.example.com/data')
```

```javascript
  .then(response => response.json())
  .then(data => {
    // Example: Update the UI with data
```

document.getElementById('dataContainer').textContent = data.message;
```javascript
  });
```

Handling Errors

Proper error handling is essential to manage issues that may arise, such as network errors or invalid responses. Implement both client-side and server-side error handling.

javascript
Copy code
```javascript
fetch('https://api.example.com/data')
  .then(response => {
    if (!response.ok) {
      throw new Error('Network response was not ok');
    }
    return response.json();
  })
  .then(data => console.log(data))
  .catch(error => {
```

```
    console.error('There was a problem with the fetch
operation:', error);
    // Display user-friendly error message
  });
```

Handling Non-JSON Responses

Some APIs may return data in formats other than JSON, such as XML or plain text. Ensure your application can handle and parse these formats appropriately.

```javascript
Copy code
fetch('https://api.example.com/data')
  .then(response => response.text()) // Parse as plain text
  .then(text => {
    console.log(text); // Process the text
  });
```

Managing Authentication and Rate Limits

APIs often require authentication and impose rate limits on the number of requests. Handle authentication errors and implement logic to manage rate limits effectively.

javascript
Copy code
```javascript
fetch('https://api.example.com/secure-data', {
  headers: {
    'Authorization': 'Bearer YOUR_ACCESS_TOKEN'
  }
})
.then(response => {
  if (response.status === 401) {
    throw new Error('Unauthorized access');
  }
  return response.json();
})
.then(data => console.log(data))
.catch(error => console.error('Error:', error));
```

Conclusion

Handling API responses involves parsing the data, managing errors, and utilizing the information effectively. By understanding the response structure, implementing robust error handling, and addressing different data formats, you can ensure that your application interacts smoothly with external APIs and provides a seamless experience for us

Chapter 11
Debugging and Error Handling

Effective debugging and error handling are crucial skills for any developer, ensuring that applications run smoothly and issues are resolved quickly. Debugging involves identifying and fixing errors or bugs in the code, while error handling focuses on anticipating potential problems and implementing strategies to manage them gracefully. Together, these practices enhance the reliability, performance, and user experience of your applications. In JavaScript, tools like console logging, breakpoints, and error objects, along with techniques for handling asynchronous errors, play a key role in maintaining robust code.

Debugging Tools and Techniques

Debugging is a critical aspect of software development that involves identifying, diagnosing, and resolving errors or bugs in your code. Various tools and techniques can help streamline this process, making it easier to find and fix issues quickly. Here's an overview of some essential debugging tools and techniques used in JavaScript development:

Debugging Tools

Console Logging

The console.log() method is one of the simplest and most commonly used debugging tools. It allows you to print variables, outputs, and messages to the browser's console, helping you track the flow and state of your application.

javascript
Copy code
console.log('This is a debug message');
console.log('Value of variable x:', x);

Browser Developer Tools

Modern browsers like Chrome, Firefox, and Edge come with built-in developer tools that provide a comprehensive suite for debugging:

Console: View log messages, errors, and interact with the JavaScript runtime.

Sources Panel: Inspect, modify, and debug JavaScript code with breakpoints, watch expressions, and call stacks.

Network Panel: Monitor network requests and responses to diagnose issues with API calls.

Elements Panel: Inspect and modify the DOM and CSS styles directly.

Breakpoints

Breakpoints allow you to pause the execution of your code at specific lines, so you can inspect variables and the call stack. This helps you understand the state of your application at various points during execution.

javascript
Copy code
```
debugger; // Manually set a breakpoint in your code
```

Watch Expressions

Watch expressions let you monitor the value of specific variables or expressions in real-time as you step through your code. This is useful for tracking how values change over time.

Call Stack

The call stack shows the sequence of function calls that led to the current point in execution. This helps you trace the flow of execution and understand how you reached a particular state.

Error Objects

JavaScript's Error object provides a way to create and throw custom error messages. You can also use built-in error types like TypeError, ReferenceError, and SyntaxError to handle specific error cases.

```javascript
Copy code
try {
    // Code that may throw an error
} catch (error) {
    console.error('An error occurred:', error.message);
}
```

Debugging Techniques

Isolate the Problem
Narrow down the section of code where the issue occurs. This can be done by systematically adding console.log() statements or using breakpoints to trace the flow of execution.

Check for Common Errors
Look for common JavaScript errors such as:

Syntax errors
Typographical errors
Incorrect function or variable usage
Asynchronous code issues (e.g., callback hell, unhandled promises)

Use Version Control

Version control systems like Git help you keep track of changes in your codebase. You can use it to revert to previous versions of your code, which is helpful when you need to identify when a bug was introduced.

Step Through Code

Use the debugging tools to step through your code line by line. This helps you understand the flow of execution and how variables change over time.

Analyze Network Requests

Use the Network panel in browser developer tools to inspect API requests and responses. Check for status codes, response data, and any errors that may occur during network communication.

Test in Different Environments

Test your application in different browsers and environments to identify issues that may be specific to a particular setup.

Automated Testing

Implement automated tests to catch errors early in the development process. Unit tests, integration tests, and end-to-end tests help ensure that your code works as expected and reduce the number of bugs in production.

Conclusion

Effective debugging requires a combination of the right tools and techniques. By leveraging console logging, browser developer tools, breakpoints, and error objects, along with systematic debugging practices, you can efficiently identify and resolve issues in your code. This ensures that your applications are robust, reliable, and provide a smooth user experience.

Handling Errors Gracefully

Handling errors gracefully is crucial in software development to ensure a robust and user-friendly application. When errors are managed effectively, they prevent the application from crashing and provide meaningful feedback to the users. Here are some key strategies and best practices for handling errors gracefully in JavaScript:

Key Strategies

Try...Catch Statements

The try...catch statement allows you to handle exceptions that may occur in a block of code. This prevents the program from crashing and lets you manage the error appropriately.

javascript
Copy code
```
try {
   // Code that may throw an error
} catch (error) {
   console.error('An error occurred:', error.message);
   // Handle the error (e.g., display a user-friendly message)
}
```

Throwing Errors

You can throw custom errors using the throw statement, providing more context about what went wrong.

javascript
Copy code
```
function validateInput(input) {
   if (!input) {
        throw new Error('Invalid input: Input cannot be empty.');
   }
   // Process the input
```

```javascript
}

try {
  validateInput('');
} catch (error) {
  console.error(error.message);
}
```

Asynchronous Error Handling

For asynchronous code, such as promises and async/await, ensure errors are properly caught and handled.

Using Promises:

javascript
Copy code
```javascript
fetch('https://api.example.com/data')
  .then(response => response.json())
  .catch(error => {
    console.error('Fetch error:', error);
  });
```
Using async/await:

javascript

```
Copy code
async function fetchData() {
    try {
                                    const   response   =   await
fetch('https://api.example.com/data');
        const data = await response.json();
        console.log(data);
    } catch (error) {
        console.error('Fetch error:', error);
    }
}

fetchData();
```

Graceful Degradation and Fallbacks
Ensure your application can still function, even if an error occurs. Provide fallbacks or default values to maintain a minimum level of functionality.

```
javascript
Copy code
function getConfig() {
    try {
        // Attempt to load config
    } catch (error) {
```

```javascript
    console.warn('Using default config due to error:', error);
    return defaultConfig; // Provide a default configuration
  }
}
```

User-Friendly Error Messages

Display meaningful and user-friendly error messages instead of technical details. This helps users understand what went wrong and what they can do next.

javascript
Copy code
```javascript
try {
  // Code that may throw an error
} catch (error) {
  alert('Something went wrong. Please try again later.');
  console.error('Detailed error information:', error);
}
```

Logging Errors

Log errors to an external service or file to monitor and analyze issues in your application. This helps in diagnosing problems and improving the code over time.

```javascript
Copy code
function logError(error) {
  // Send error details to a logging service
}

try {
  // Code that may throw an error
} catch (error) {
  logError(error);
  console.error('An error occurred:', error);
}
```

Validating Inputs

Prevent errors by validating inputs before processing them. This helps catch potential issues early and provides immediate feedback to users.

```javascript
Copy code
function processInput(input) {
  if (typeof input !== 'string') {
    throw new TypeError('Expected a string input');
```

```
  }
  // Process the input
}

try {
  processInput(42);
} catch (error) {
  console.error(error.message);
}
```

Conclusion

Handling errors gracefully is essential for creating resilient and user-friendly applications. By using try...catch statements, managing asynchronous errors, providing fallbacks, displaying user-friendly messages, logging errors, and validating inputs, you can ensure that your application handles issues effectively and maintains a positive user experience.

Writing Testable Code

Writing testable code is essential for creating robust and maintainable software. Testable code is designed to be easily verified through automated tests, ensuring that each component functions correctly and integrates seamlessly with others. Here's how to write code that is both easy to test and reliable:

Key Principles

Modular Design

Small Functions: Break down large functions into smaller, single-purpose functions. Smaller functions are easier to test in isolation and make it simpler to understand the code's behavior.

javascript
Copy code

```javascript
// Example of modular code
function calculateTotal(items) {
    return items.reduce((total, item) => total + item.price, 0);
}

function applyDiscount(total, discount) {
```

```javascript
    return total - (total * discount);
}
```

Single Responsibility Principle

Focused Functions: Ensure that each function or class has only one responsibility or task. This makes it easier to test individual components and maintain the code.

javascript

Copy code

```javascript
// Example of single responsibility
function fetchUserData(userId) {
    return fetch(`https://api.example.com/users/${userId}`)
        .then(response => response.json());
}

function formatUserData(userData) {
    return `${userData.firstName} ${userData.lastName}`;
}
```

Dependency Injection

Inject Dependencies: Pass dependencies (such as services or configuration) into functions or classes rather than hardcoding them. This allows for easier testing and mocking of dependencies.

javascript
Copy code

```javascript
// Example of dependency injection
function fetchData(fetchFunction) {
    return fetchFunction('https://api.example.com/data');
}

// In tests
fetchData(() => Promise.resolve({ data: 'test' }));
```

Pure Functions

Avoid Side Effects: Write pure functions that do not modify external state or depend on external variables. Pure functions produce the same output for the same input, making them easier to test.

.

javascript
Copy code

```javascript
// Pure function example
function multiply(a, b) {
    return a * b;
}
```

Error Handling

Graceful Error Management: Implement clear and consistent error handling. Test how your code handles different types of errors and edge cases to ensure robustness.

javascript

Copy code

```javascript
function divide(a, b) {
  if (b === 0) {
    throw new Error('Division by zero');
  }
  return a / b;
}
```

Test Coverage

Unit Tests: Write unit tests to verify that individual functions and modules work as expected.

Integration Tests: Test interactions between different parts of your application to ensure they work together correctly.

End-to-End Tests: Simulate real user scenarios to test the entire application workflow from start to finish.

javascript

Copy code

```
// Example of a unit test
describe('multiply function', () => {
  it('should return the product of two numbers', () => {
    expect(multiply(2, 3)).toBe(6);
  });
});
```

Mocking and Stubbing

Simulate Dependencies: Use mocks and stubs to simulate the behavior of external services or components during tests. This isolates the unit under test and controls the test environment.

javascript
Copy code

```
// Example of mocking
jest.mock('axios');
axios.get.mockResolvedValue({ data: 'test' });
```

Readable and Maintainable Code

Descriptive Naming: Use clear, descriptive names for functions and variables to make the code easier to understand and test.

Consistent Style: Follow coding standards and conventions to improve readability and maintainability.

javascript
Copy code

```javascript
// Readable code example
function calculateDiscountedPrice(price, discount) {
    return price - (price * discount);
}
```

Conclusion

Writing testable code involves creating modular, single-responsibility functions, using dependency injection, avoiding side effects, and implementing robust error handling. By focusing on these principles, you make your code more reliable, maintainable, and easier to test, which contributes to a more stable and efficient development process.

Chapter 12
Modern JavaScript (ES6 and Beyond)

Modern JavaScript, introduced with ES6 (ECMAScript 2015) and subsequent versions, brings a host of new features and enhancements that significantly improve the language's functionality, readability, and developer experience. These updates include new syntax, data structures, and built-in methods that simplify complex tasks, enhance code maintainability, and facilitate more efficient development practices. With features such as arrow functions, classes, template literals, and async/await, modern JavaScript empowers developers to write cleaner, more expressive code and build robust applications with ease. Embracing these advancements is key to leveraging the full potential of JavaScript in today's development landscape.

New Features in ES6

ECMAScript 2015 (commonly known as ES6) introduced several powerful features that enhance the capabilities of JavaScript. These new features improve code readability, maintainability, and functionality. Here's an overview of some of the most significant additions in ES6:

1. Let and Const

let: Introduces block-scoped variables, providing a more predictable way to handle variable scope compared to var, which is function-scoped.
const: Declares block-scoped variables whose values cannot be reassigned. It ensures that constants remain immutable.

```javascript
Copy code
let name = 'John';
name = 'Doe'; // Allowed

const pi = 3.14;
pi = 3.14159; // Error: Assignment to constant variable
```

2. Arrow Functions

Provide a concise syntax for writing functions. They also inherit the this context from their surrounding scope, which simplifies handling of this in callbacks.

javascript
Copy code
```
// Traditional function
function add(a, b) {
    return a + b;
}


// Arrow function
const add = (a, b) => a + b;
```

3. Template Literals

Allow for multi-line strings and string interpolation using backticks (`). They make it easier to construct complex strings and embed expressions.

javascript
Copy code
```
const name = 'Alice';
const message = `Hello, ${name}!`;
```

4. Destructuring Assignment

Provides a way to unpack values from arrays or properties from objects into distinct variables, simplifying the process of accessing multiple properties or elements.

javascript
Copy code
```
// Array destructuring
const [a, b] = [1, 2];

// Object destructuring
const { name, age } = { name: 'Bob', age: 30 };
```

5. Default Parameters

Allows functions to have default values for parameters, which are used if no arguments or undefined are passed.
javascript
Copy code
```
function greet(name = 'Guest') {
   return `Hello, ${name}!`;
}
```

6. Rest and Spread Operators

Rest Operator: Collects multiple arguments into an array, useful for functions with variable numbers of parameters.
Spread Operator: Expands an array into individual elements, useful for function arguments and array copying.

javascript
Copy code

```
// Rest operator
function sum(...numbers) {
    return numbers.reduce((total, num) => total + num, 0);
}

// Spread operator
const arr = [1, 2, 3];
const newArr = [...arr, 4, 5];
```

7. Classes

Introduces a class syntax for creating objects and handling inheritance. This syntax is more familiar to developers from object-oriented programming backgrounds.
javascript
Copy code

```javascript
class Person {
  constructor(name, age) {
    this.name = name;
    this.age = age;
  }

  greet() {
    return `Hello, my name is ${this.name}`;
  }
}

const person = new Person('Eve', 25);
```

8. Modules

ES6 modules provide a standardized way to export and import code between files, improving code organization and reusability.
javascript
Copy code

```javascript
// lib.js
export const pi = 3.14;
export function add(a, b) {
  return a + b;
}
```

```javascript
// app.js
import { pi, add } from './lib.js';
```

9. Promises

Provide a way to handle asynchronous operations more effectively, enabling chaining and better management of asynchronous code.

javascript

Copy code

```javascript
const fetchData = () => {
  return new Promise((resolve, reject) => {
    // Asynchronous operation
    if (/* success */) {
      resolve(data);
    } else {
      reject(error);
    }
  });
};
```

```javascript
fetchData().then(data => console.log(data)).catch(error => console.error(error));
```

10. Symbol

A new primitive data type used to create unique identifiers for object properties, avoiding name collisions.

javascript

Copy code

```javascript
const uniqueSymbol = Symbol('description');
const obj = {
  [uniqueSymbol]: 'value'
};
```

Conclusion

ES6 introduced a range of features that modernize JavaScript and make it more powerful and expressive. By leveraging these features, developers can write cleaner, more efficient code, handle asynchronous operations more gracefully, and better organize their code into modules. Understanding and using these features effectively is crucial for working with contemporary JavaScript and developing advanced web applications.

Using Modules

Modules in JavaScript are a way to organize and encapsulate code, making it easier to manage and maintain complex applications. They allow developers to split code into smaller, reusable pieces that can be imported and exported between different files. This modular approach enhances code readability, promotes reuse, and simplifies dependency management. Here's an overview of how to use modules in JavaScript:

1. Introduction to Modules

Modules enable you to define and use code in a modular fashion. They help in breaking down large applications into smaller, more manageable pieces. JavaScript modules use export and import statements to share and consume code between different files.

2. Exporting Modules

To make code available for use in other files, you need to export it. There are two primary types of exports: named exports and default exports.

Named Exports: Allow you to export multiple items from a module. Each exported item must be imported with the same name in the importing file.

javascript
Copy code
```
// math.js
export const add = (a, b) => a + b;
export const subtract = (a, b) => a - b;
```

Default Exports: Allow you to export a single value or function from a module. The importing file can use any name to import this default export.

javascript
Copy code
```
// greet.js
const greet = name => `Hello, ${name}!`;
export default greet;
```

3. Importing Modules

To use exported functionality in another file, you need to import it. You can import named and default exports in the following ways:

Importing Named Exports: Use curly braces to specify which items you want to import.

```javascript
Copy code
// app.js
import { add, subtract } from './math.js';

console.log(add(2, 3)); // 5
console.log(subtract(5, 3)); // 2
```

Importing Default Exports: Import the default export without curly braces. You can name the import whatever you like.

```javascript
Copy code
// app.js
import greet from './greet.js';

console.log(greet('Alice')); // Hello, Alice!
```

4. Combining Named and Default Exports

A module can have both named and default exports. You can import them together in a single import statement.

```javascript
Copy code
// utils.js
export const multiply = (a, b) => a * b;
export const divide = (a, b) => a / b;
export default function calculate(a, b) {
    return a + b;
}

// app.js
import calculate, { multiply, divide } from './utils.js';

console.log(calculate(2, 3)); // 5
console.log(multiply(2, 3)); // 6
console.log(divide(6, 3)); // 2
```

5. Dynamic Imports

Dynamic imports allow you to load modules asynchronously, which can be useful for optimizing performance by loading code only when needed.

```javascript
Copy code
// app.js
async function loadModule() {
    const module = await import('./math.js');
    console.log(module.add(2, 3)); // 5
}

loadModule();
```

6. Module File Extensions

In most modern JavaScript environments, modules use .js or .mjs file extensions. When using .mjs, the file is treated as a module by default. In environments that support ES modules natively (like Node.js or modern browsers), the .js extension can also be used.

7. Module Resolution and Path
Modules are resolved relative to the importing file's location. For example, import { add } from './math.js'; looks for

math.js in the same directory as the importing file. You can also use relative paths to navigate to different directories.

Conclusion

JavaScript modules provide a powerful way to organize and manage code by encapsulating functionality into reusable components. Using export and import statements, you can create modular, maintainable applications that are easier to understand and debug. Embracing modules is essential for developing modern JavaScript applications and leveraging the full capabilities of the language.

Transpiling with Babel

Babel is a widely used tool that enables developers to use modern JavaScript features while ensuring compatibility with older browsers and environments. It serves as a JavaScript compiler that transforms code written in newer ECMAScript versions or using experimental features into a version of JavaScript that can run in a wider range of environments. This process is known as transpiling. Here's an overview of how Babel works and why it's essential for modern web development:

1. What is Babel?

Babel is an open-source JavaScript transpiler that converts modern JavaScript (ES6 and beyond) into a more widely supported version of JavaScript. It allows developers to use the latest language features without worrying about browser compatibility issues.

2. Why Use Babel?

Compatibility: Ensure that your JavaScript code runs in older browsers and environments that do not support the latest ECMAScript features.
Future-Proofing: Write code using future JavaScript syntax and features, knowing that Babel will handle the necessary transformations.
Consistency: Maintain a consistent development experience by using the latest JavaScript features, regardless of the runtime environment.

3. How Babel Works

Babel operates in several stages:

Parsing: Babel parses your JavaScript code into an Abstract Syntax Tree (AST). This tree represents the structure of your code in a format that Babel can understand and manipulate.

Transformation: Babel applies plugins to the AST to transform modern syntax into equivalent code that is compatible with older JavaScript environments. For example, it can convert ES6 arrow functions into ES5 function expressions.

Code Generation: Babel generates the transformed code from the updated AST, producing the final output that will be executed by the JavaScript engine.

4. Setting Up Babel

To use Babel in your project, you typically follow these steps:

Install Babel: Add Babel and its required packages to your project using a package manager like npm or Yarn.

bash

Copy code

npm install --save-dev @babel/core @babel/cli @babel/preset-env

Configure Babel: Create a Babel configuration file (.babelrc or babel.config.json) to specify which presets and plugins to use.

json

Copy code

```json
{
  "presets": ["@babel/preset-env"]
}
```

@babel/preset-env: A preset that includes a collection of plugins to convert modern JavaScript features into compatible code based on the target environment.

Add Build Scripts: Define build scripts in your package.json to run Babel and transpile your code.

json

Copy code

```json
"scripts": {
```

```
    "build": "babel src --out-dir lib"
}
```
src: The directory containing your modern JavaScript source code.

lib: The directory where the transpiled code will be output.

Run Babel: Execute the build script to transpile your code.

```bash
Copy code
npm run build
```

5. Babel Plugins and Presets

Plugins: Extend Babel's functionality by transforming specific features or syntax. Examples include @babel/plugin-transform-arrow-functions for converting arrow functions.

Presets: Collections of plugins bundled together to handle a set of transformations. Common presets include @babel/preset-env for general ECMAScript features and @babel/preset-react for React JSX.

6. Integrating Babel with Build Tools

Babel is often used in conjunction with build tools like Webpack, Parcel, or Rollup. These tools can be configured to use Babel during the build process, enabling seamless integration into modern development workflows.

```javascript
Copy code
// Example Webpack configuration
module.exports = {
  module: {
    rules: [
      {
        test: /\.js$/,
        exclude: /node_modules/,
        use: {
          loader: 'babel-loader',
          options: {
            presets: ['@babel/preset-env']
          }
        }
      }
    ]
  }
};
```

7. Babel and Polyfills

While Babel transforms syntax, it doesn't automatically polyfill new APIs (like Promise or Array.prototype.includes). Use the @babel/polyfill or core-js library to add polyfills for these features.

bash
Copy code
npm install core-js

javascript
Copy code
// Import polyfills at the entry point of your application
import 'core-js/stable';
import 'regenerator-runtime/runtime';

Conclusion

Babel is an essential tool for modern JavaScript development, enabling developers to use the latest language features while maintaining compatibility with a broad range of environments. By transpiling code with Babel, you ensure that your applications are accessible to users regardless of their browser or JavaScript engine, allowing you to leverage the full power of contemporary JavaScript.

Chapter 13
Building Interactive Web Pages

Building interactive web pages involves creating engaging user experiences that respond to user actions and inputs. By leveraging HTML for structure, CSS for styling, and JavaScript for dynamic behavior, developers can craft web pages that are not only visually appealing but also responsive and functional. This integration allows for interactive elements such as forms, buttons, and animations, which enhance user engagement and make web applications more intuitive and enjoyable to use.

Enhancing User Experience with JavaScript

Enhancing user experience (UX) with JavaScript involves adding dynamic and interactive features to a web page that improve usability and engagement. JavaScript enables developers to create responsive, intuitive interfaces that react

275

to user actions in real time. Here's how JavaScript can be used to enhance UX:

1. Interactive Elements

JavaScript allows you to add interactive components to your web pages, such as:

Forms and Validation: Implement real-time form validation to provide immediate feedback on user input, ensuring data accuracy and improving user satisfaction.

```javascript
Copy code
const form = document.getElementById('contact-form');
form.addEventListener('submit', (event) => {
  const name = document.getElementById('name').value;
  if (name === '') {
    alert('Name is required');
    event.preventDefault(); // Prevent form submission
  }
});
```

Buttons and Click Events: Enhance buttons with event listeners to trigger actions like showing/hiding content, changing styles, or navigating to different sections.

javascript
Copy code
```javascript
const button = document.getElementById('toggle-button');
button.addEventListener('click', () => {
    const content = document.getElementById('content');
    content.style.display = content.style.display === 'none' ?
'block' : 'none';
});
```

2. Dynamic Content Updates

JavaScript enables the dynamic updating of content without requiring a page reload. This can be achieved through:

AJAX Requests: Use AJAX (Asynchronous JavaScript and XML) to fetch data from the server and update parts of the web page dynamically.

javascript
Copy code
```javascript
const loadContent = () => {
```

```javascript
fetch('https://api.example.com/data')
  .then(response => response.json())
  .then(data => {

document.getElementById('data-container').innerText   =
data.message;
    });
};
```

DOM Manipulation: Modify the DOM (Document Object Model) to add, remove, or update elements based on user interactions or data changes.

```javascript
javascript
Copy code
const addItem = (item) => {
  const list = document.getElementById('item-list');
  const listItem = document.createElement('li');
  listItem.textContent = item;
  list.appendChild(listItem);
};
```

3. Animations and Transitions

Enhance visual appeal and guide user interactions with animations and transitions. JavaScript can control CSS animations or create animations directly.

CSS Transitions: Use JavaScript to trigger CSS transitions for smooth visual effects, such as fading elements in and out.

javascript
Copy code

```javascript
const element = document.getElementById('fade');
element.addEventListener('click', () => {
    element.style.transition = 'opacity 0.5s';
    element.style.opacity = '0';
});
```

Canvas and SVG Animations: Create complex animations and graphics using the Canvas API or SVG (Scalable Vector Graphics) with JavaScript.

javascript
Copy code

```javascript
const canvas = document.getElementById('myCanvas');
const ctx = canvas.getContext('2d');
ctx.fillStyle = 'blue';
ctx.fillRect(10, 10, 100, 100);
```

4. User Feedback

Provide feedback to users based on their actions to improve interaction clarity:

Alerts and Notifications: Use JavaScript to display alerts, notifications, or confirmations to inform users about the results of their actions.

javascript
Copy code

```javascript
alert('Your form has been submitted successfully!');
```

Tooltips and Popups: Show additional information or guidance with tooltips and popups that appear on hover or click.

javascript
Copy code

```javascript
const tooltip = document.getElementById('tooltip');
document.getElementById('hover-element').addEventListener('mouseover', () => {
   tooltip.style.display = 'block';
});
```

```javascript
document.getElementById('hover-element').addEventListe
ner('mouseout', () => {
  tooltip.style.display = 'none';
});
```

5. Responsive Design

JavaScript can enhance responsive design by adapting content and layout based on user interactions or screen size changes.

Responsive Menus: Create navigation menus that adjust their appearance and functionality for different screen sizes or orientations.

javascript
Copy code
```javascript
const menuButton = document.getElementById('menu-button');
menuButton.addEventListener('click', () => {
  const menu = document.getElementById('menu');
  menu.classList.toggle('active');
});
```

Conclusion

JavaScript plays a crucial role in enhancing user experience by making web pages interactive, dynamic, and responsive. Through interactive elements, dynamic content updates, animations, user feedback, and responsive design, JavaScript helps create engaging and intuitive user experiences that keep visitors satisfied and coming back.

Creating Interactive Elements

Creating interactive elements on a web page involves using JavaScript to make the page respond to user actions in real-time. These elements can range from simple buttons to complex dynamic interfaces. The goal is to enhance user engagement by providing immediate feedback and interactive features. Here's how you can create interactive elements using JavaScript:

1. Buttons and Click Events

Buttons are a fundamental interactive element. JavaScript can be used to attach event listeners to buttons, allowing them to perform actions when clicked.

Basic Button Interaction: Attach an event listener to a button to execute a function when the button is clicked.

html
Copy code
```
<button id="click-me">Click Me</button>
<script>
  const button = document.getElementById('click-me');
  button.addEventListener('click', () => {
    alert('Button was clicked!');
  });
</script>
```

2. Forms and Input Handling

Forms are used to collect user input. JavaScript can validate form data, handle user submissions, and dynamically update form elements.

Form Validation: Validate user input before submission to ensure data integrity and provide instant feedback.

html
Copy code

```
<form id="my-form">
    <input type="text" id="name" placeholder="Enter your name">
  <input type="submit" value="Submit">
</form>
<script>

document.getElementById('my-form').addEventListener('submit', (event) => {
    const name = document.getElementById('name').value;
    if (name === '') {
      alert('Name cannot be empty!');
      event.preventDefault(); // Prevent form submission
    }
  });
</script>
```

3. Modals and Popups

Modals and popups provide additional information or require user interaction without navigating away from the current page.

Creating a Modal: Display a modal dialog when a button is clicked and hide it when the user closes it.

html
Copy code

```html
<button id="open-modal">Open Modal</button>
<div id="my-modal" style="display: none;">
  <div class="modal-content">
    <span id="close-modal">&times;</span>
    <p>This is a modal popup!</p>
  </div>
</div>
<script>
                const openModalButton = document.getElementById('open-modal');
  const modal = document.getElementById('my-modal');
                const closeModalButton = document.getElementById('close-modal');

  openModalButton.addEventListener('click', () => {
    modal.style.display = 'block';
```

```javascript
});

closeModalButton.addEventListener('click', () => {
  modal.style.display = 'none';
});

window.addEventListener('click', (event) => {
  if (event.target === modal) {
    modal.style.display = 'none';
  }
});
```
</script>

4. Tabs and Accordions

Tabs and accordions organize content into collapsible sections or tabs, enhancing navigation and user experience.

Tabs: Switch between different content sections by clicking on tabs.

html
Copy code
```html
<div class="tabs">
```

```
  <button class="tab-button" data-target="tab1">Tab
1</button>
  <button class="tab-button" data-target="tab2">Tab
2</button>
</div>
<div id="tab1" class="tab-content">Content for Tab
1</div>
<div id="tab2" class="tab-content" style="display:
none;">Content for Tab 2</div>
<script>

document.querySelectorAll('.tab-button').forEach(button
=> {
    button.addEventListener('click', () => {

document.querySelectorAll('.tab-content').forEach(content
=> {
        content.style.display = 'none';
      });

document.getElementById(button.getAttribute('data-targe
t')).style.display = 'block';
    });
  });
</script>
```

Accordions: Expand and collapse sections of content to show or hide information.

html
Copy code

```
<button class="accordion">Section 1</button>
<div class="panel">
  <p>Content for Section 1.</p>
</div>
<button class="accordion">Section 2</button>
<div class="panel">
  <p>Content for Section 2.</p>
</div>
<script>
  document.querySelectorAll('.accordion').forEach(button => {
    button.addEventListener('click', () => {
      const panel = button.nextElementSibling;
      if (panel.style.display === 'block') {
        panel.style.display = 'none';
      } else {
        panel.style.display = 'block';
      }
    });
  });
```

```
</script>
```

5. Dynamic Content Updates

JavaScript can dynamically update the content of a page without reloading, creating a more fluid and interactive experience.

Updating Content: Change the content of a page element in response to user actions or data changes.

html
Copy code

```
<button id="update-content">Update Content</button>
<p id="content">Original content</p>
<script>

document.getElementById('update-content').addEventListener('click', () => {
        document.getElementById('content').textContent =
'Content has been updated!';
   });
</script>
```

Conclusion

Creating interactive elements with JavaScript enhances user engagement by making web pages more responsive and dynamic. From handling button clicks and form submissions to managing modals, tabs, and dynamic content updates, JavaScript provides the tools needed to build interactive and user-friendly web applications. By integrating these interactive elements, you can create a more engaging and effective user experience.

Animations and Transitions

Animations and transitions are crucial for creating engaging and visually appealing web experiences. They help make interfaces feel more dynamic and responsive, guiding users' attention and enhancing usability. JavaScript, along with CSS, is often used to create these effects, providing a richer user experience. Here's an overview of how to use animations and transitions effectively:

1. CSS Transitions

CSS transitions allow you to change property values smoothly over a specified duration. They are ideal for simple effects like fading, sliding, or resizing elements.

Basic Transition Example: Smoothly change an element's background color when it is hovered over.

html
Copy code
```
<style>
  .box {
    width: 100px;
    height: 100px;
    background-color: blue;
    transition: background-color 0.5s ease;
  }
  .box:hover {
    background-color: red;
  }
</style>
<div class="box"></div>
```

Transition Properties: Customize transitions by specifying properties such as transition-property, transition-duration, transition-timing-function, and transition-delay.

css
Copy code

```css
.box {
    transition-property: background-color, transform;
    transition-duration: 0.5s, 1s;
    transition-timing-function: ease, linear;
}
```

2. CSS Animations

CSS animations provide more control and complexity compared to transitions. They involve defining keyframes that specify the start and end states of an animation and the intermediate waypoints.

Basic Animation Example: Create a simple animation that moves an element from left to right.

html
Copy code

```html
<style>
  @keyframes moveRight {
    from { transform: translateX(0); }
```

```css
    to { transform: translateX(100px); }
  }
  .animated-box {
    width: 100px;
    height: 100px;
    background-color: blue;
    animation: moveRight 2s infinite alternate;
  }
</style>
<div class="animated-box"></div>
```

Keyframe Properties: Define keyframes using percentages or keywords (from and to) to describe how the CSS properties should change over time.

css
Copy code

```css
@keyframes slide {
  0% { opacity: 0; transform: translateX(-100%); }
  50% { opacity: 0.5; transform: translateX(0); }
  100% { opacity: 1; transform: translateX(100%); }
}
```

3. JavaScript-Driven Animations

JavaScript can be used to create more complex or interactive animations. Libraries like GreenSock (GSAP) or frameworks like anime.js simplify animating multiple elements and handling animations with more precision.

Using JavaScript for Animations: Trigger animations based on user interactions or other events.

```html
Copy code
<style>
  .box {
    width: 100px;
    height: 100px;
    background-color: blue;
    position: relative;
  }
</style>
<div class="box" id="animate-box"></div>
<script>

document.getElementById('animate-box').addEventListener('click', () => {
    const box = document.getElementById('animate-box');
    box.style.transition = 'transform 1s';
```

```
    box.style.transform = 'translateX(200px)';
  });
</script>
```

Using Animation Libraries: Leverage libraries to simplify complex animations and handle multiple properties.

```html
Copy code
<script
src="https://cdn.jsdelivr.net/npm/animejs@3.2.1/lib/anime
.min.js"></script>
<script>
  anime({
    targets: '.box',
    translateX: 250,
    duration: 2000,
    easing: 'easeInOutQuad'
  });
</script>
```

4. Best Practices

Performance Considerations: Use hardware-accelerated properties like transform and opacity for smoother animations. Avoid animating properties that trigger layout changes, such as width and height.

Accessibility: Ensure that animations do not hinder accessibility. Provide options to disable animations for users who may experience motion sensitivity.

Consistency: Maintain consistent animation styles across your application to create a cohesive user experience.

Conclusion
Animations and transitions play a key role in creating engaging and user-friendly web experiences. By leveraging CSS transitions and animations, along with JavaScript for more complex interactions, you can add visual interest and improve the overall usability of your web applications. Balancing aesthetic appeal with performance and accessibility ensures that animations enhance the user experience without detracting from it.

Chapter 14
Introduction to JavaScript Frameworks

JavaScript frameworks are powerful tools that help developers build complex web applications more efficiently and effectively. They provide pre-written code and structures for common tasks, such as DOM manipulation, event handling, and state management, allowing developers to focus on unique features rather than reinventing the wheel.

Frameworks like React, Angular, and Vue.js have become popular due to their ability to streamline the development process, enforce best practices, and create maintainable codebases. React, developed by Facebook, is known for its component-based architecture and virtual DOM. Angular, by Google, offers a comprehensive suite for building single-page applications with features like two-way data binding and dependency injection. Vue.js, designed by Evan You, combines the best aspects of both React and Angular, providing a flexible and progressive framework that's easy to integrate and scale.

Choosing the right framework depends on your project's requirements, the learning curve, and the available community support. Using JavaScript frameworks can significantly enhance productivity, performance, and the overall user experience of your web applications.

Overview of Popular Frameworks (React, Vue, Angular)

JavaScript frameworks have revolutionized web development by providing powerful tools for building dynamic, scalable applications. Among the most popular frameworks are React, Vue, and Angular. Each offers unique features and advantages, catering to different project needs and developer preferences.

React
Developed by: Facebook

Key Features:

Component-Based Architecture: React structures applications using reusable components, promoting modularity and maintainability.

Virtual DOM: React uses a virtual DOM to efficiently update and render UI components, enhancing performance. JSX Syntax: React combines JavaScript with HTML-like syntax (JSX), making the code more intuitive and easier to write.

Unidirectional Data Flow: React enforces a one-way data flow, simplifying state management and debugging.
Use Cases: React is ideal for building complex single-page applications (SPAs) and user interfaces that require frequent updates. It is widely used in social media platforms, e-commerce sites, and content management systems.

```jsx
Copy code
import React from 'react';
import ReactDOM from 'react-dom';

function App() {
    return <h1>Hello, World!</h1>;
}
```

```
ReactDOM.render(<App                          />,
document.getElementById('root'));
```
Vue.js
Developed by: Evan You

Key Features:

Progressive Framework: Vue is designed to be incrementally adoptable. You can use as much or as little of it as needed.

Reactive Data Binding: Vue's reactivity system ensures that the UI automatically updates when the underlying data changes.

Component-Based Architecture: Like React, Vue uses components to build user interfaces.
Single-File Components: Vue components can include HTML, CSS, and JavaScript in a single file, promoting separation of concerns and ease of development.

Use Cases: Vue is versatile and can be used for anything from small, interactive components to full-fledged SPAs. It's particularly popular for its simplicity and flexibility, making it a good choice for developers new to modern JavaScript frameworks.

```html
Copy code
<div id="app">{{ message }}</div>

<script>
  new Vue({
    el: '#app',
    data: {
      message: 'Hello, World!'
    }
  });
</script>
```

Angular

Developed by: Google

Key Features:

Comprehensive Framework: Angular offers a full suite of tools and libraries for building SPAs, including powerful templating, dependency injection, and built-in routing.

Two-Way Data Binding: Angular's two-way data binding automatically synchronizes data between the model and the view, reducing the amount of boilerplate code.

TypeScript Support: Angular is built with TypeScript, providing strong typing and advanced features that improve code quality and maintainability.

Modular Architecture: Angular's modular design allows developers to organize code into modules, enhancing scalability and reusability.

Use Cases: Angular is well-suited for large-scale enterprise applications where a robust structure and comprehensive toolset are needed. It's commonly used in complex business applications, enterprise-level software, and large SPAs.

```typescript
Copy code
import { Component } from '@angular/core';

@Component({
  selector: 'app-root',
  template: '<h1>Hello, World!</h1>'
})
export class AppComponent {}
```

Conclusion

React, Vue, and Angular each offer distinct advantages tailored to different development needs. React excels in performance and simplicity with its virtual DOM and JSX syntax. Vue stands out for its progressive nature and ease of integration, making it accessible for beginners and flexible for experienced developers. Angular provides a comprehensive, all-in-one solution ideal for large-scale applications, offering robust features and strong typing with TypeScript. Understanding the strengths of each framework can help you choose the best tool for your project, ensuring efficient development and maintainable, high-quality code.

Deciding When to Use a Framework

Choosing whether to use a JavaScript framework and selecting the right one can significantly impact the efficiency and success of your web development project. Here's a guide

303

to help you decide when to use a framework and which factors to consider:

When to Use a Framework

1. Complexity of the Project

Complex Applications: If your project involves complex user interfaces, dynamic content updates, or single-page applications (SPAs), using a framework can simplify development and maintenance.
Simple Websites: For static websites or simple projects with minimal interactivity, using a framework might be overkill. Basic JavaScript or even plain HTML and CSS might suffice.

2. Development Speed and Efficiency

Rapid Development: Frameworks provide pre-built components, tools, and best practices, accelerating development time. They allow you to focus on building features rather than solving common problems from scratch.
Prototype and MVP: When developing a prototype or minimum viable product (MVP), a framework can help you

quickly create a functional application that you can iterate on.

3. Team Collaboration

Large Teams: Frameworks enforce a consistent code structure and conventions, making it easier for multiple developers to work on the same project without creating conflicting code.
Onboarding New Developers: Well-documented frameworks with strong community support can make it easier to onboard new developers and ensure they follow best practices.

4. Scalability and Maintainability

Long-Term Projects: For projects expected to grow and evolve over time, frameworks provide a scalable architecture and modular design, which helps in maintaining and extending the application.
Code Maintenance: Frameworks promote reusable code and modularity, making it easier to manage and update your codebase as the project grows.

Factors to Consider When Choosing a Framework

1. Project Requirements

Specific Needs: Evaluate the specific needs of your project, such as performance, SEO, interactivity, and real-time updates. Choose a framework that aligns with these requirements.

2. Learning Curve

Team Expertise: Consider your team's familiarity with different frameworks. Some frameworks have steeper learning curves than others. For example, Angular might require more upfront learning compared to Vue.
Documentation and Community Support: A framework with extensive documentation and an active community can help reduce the learning curve and provide support when needed.

3. Ecosystem and Tooling

Third-Party Libraries and Plugins: A strong ecosystem with a variety of plugins and libraries can extend the functionality of your framework and simplify integration with other tools.

Development Tools: Consider the availability of development tools such as debugging, testing, and build tools that can enhance your development workflow.

4. Performance

Rendering Efficiency: Evaluate the performance characteristics of the framework, such as how it handles DOM updates and data binding. Frameworks like React with its virtual DOM are optimized for performance.
Bundle Size: Consider the size of the framework and its impact on the initial load time of your application. Lightweight frameworks can improve performance, especially for users with slower connections.

5. Future-Proofing

Longevity and Updates: Choose a framework with an active development community and regular updates to ensure long-term support and the adoption of new web standards.
Backward Compatibility: Ensure that the framework maintains backward compatibility, allowing you to update the framework without breaking your existing codebase.

Conclusion

Deciding when to use a JavaScript framework depends on the complexity, scalability, and specific needs of your project. Frameworks like React, Vue, and Angular offer powerful tools and structures that can enhance development efficiency, maintainability, and scalability. By considering factors such as project requirements, learning curve, ecosystem, performance, and future-proofing, you can make an informed decision on whether to use a framework and which one to choose, ensuring a successful and efficient development process.

Getting Started with a Framework

Embarking on a project using a JavaScript framework can streamline development and enhance your application's functionality. Here's a step-by-step guide to help you get started with a framework:

1. Select the Right Framework

Choosing the appropriate framework depends on your project's requirements and your team's familiarity. Popular frameworks include:

React: Ideal for building complex, interactive UIs with reusable components and a virtual DOM.

Vue.js: Known for its flexibility and ease of integration, suitable for both small and large applications.

Angular: A comprehensive framework offering a full suite of tools for large-scale applications with TypeScript support.

2. Set Up Your Development Environment

Install Node.js and npm
Most JavaScript frameworks rely on Node.js and npm for managing dependencies and running build tools.

Download and Install Node.js from nodejs.org.
Verify Installation:
bash
Copy code

node -v

npm -v

Create a New Project

Use the framework's CLI or package manager to initialize your project.

React:

```bash
Copy code
npx create-react-app my-app
cd my-app
npm start
```

Vue.js:

```bash
Copy code
npm install -g @vue/cli
vue create my-app
cd my-app
npm run serve
```

Angular:

```bash
Copy code
npm install -g @angular/cli
ng new my-app
cd my-app
ng serve
```

3. Understand the Project Structure
Familiarize yourself with the typical project structure of your chosen framework:

React:

src/: Contains source code, including components and styles.
public/: Static files such as index.html.
node_modules/: Dependencies.

Vue.js:

src/: Main source directory with components and views.
public/: Static assets.
node_modules/: Dependencies.

Angular:

src/: Application source files and modules.

app/: Core components and services.

node_modules/: Dependencies.

4. Learn the Basics

React

Components: Building blocks of React applications, written as functions or classes.

```jsx
Copy code
function App() {
  return <h1>Hello, World!</h1>;
}
```

JSX: Syntax extension that allows you to write HTML-like code within JavaScript.

Vue.js

Components: Single-file components that include <template>, <script>, and <style>.

vue
Copy code

```vue
<template>
  <h1>Hello, World!</h1>
</template>
<script>
export default {
  name: 'App'
}
</script>
```

Directives: Special syntax for binding data to the DOM.

html
Copy code

```html
<p v-if="isVisible">Visible content</p>
```

Angular

Components: Class-based components with decorators, integrating templates and styles.

typescript
Copy code

```typescript
@Component({
```

```typescript
  selector: 'app-root',
  template: '<h1>Hello, World!</h1>',
})
export class AppComponent {}
```

Modules: Organize application code into functional units.

typescript
Copy code
```typescript
@NgModule({
  declarations: [AppComponent],
  imports: [BrowserModule],
  bootstrap: [AppComponent],
})
export class AppModule {}
```

.5. Build Your Application

Start developing your application by creating components, setting up routing, and managing state. Follow the framework's best practices:

React: Use state hooks (useState) and effect hooks (useEffect) for managing component state and side effects.

Vue.js: Utilize Vue's reactive properties and lifecycle hooks.
Angular: Leverage Angular services for managing data and business logic.

6. Utilize Development Tools

React DevTools: For inspecting and debugging React components.
Vue Devtools: For debugging Vue applications and inspecting component states.
Angular DevTools: For performance profiling and debugging Angular apps.

7. Follow Best Practices

Code Organization: Maintain modular and well-structured code.
Version Control: Use Git for source code management and collaboration.
Testing: Write unit and integration tests to ensure code quality.
Performance Optimization: Implement code splitting, lazy loading, and efficient state management.

Conclusion

Getting started with a JavaScript framework involves selecting the right tool, setting up your development environment, understanding the framework's structure, and following best practices. By mastering these steps, you can efficiently build and scale web applications, leveraging the framework's capabilities to enhance development speed and application performance.

Chapter 15
Best Practices and Coding Standards

Adhering to best practices and coding standards is crucial for writing maintainable, scalable, and high-quality JavaScript code. These practices not only improve code readability and consistency but also enhance collaboration among developers and streamline the debugging and testing processes. By following established guidelines and standards, you ensure that your codebase remains clean, efficient, and easy to manage as your project evolves.

Introduction

In the fast-paced world of web development, where technologies and frameworks are continually advancing, establishing best practices and coding standards is essential. These guidelines help developers produce code that is both functional and maintainable, ensuring that software projects meet high-quality standards and can be easily understood and modified by others.

Best practices cover a wide range of topics, including code structure, naming conventions, error handling, performance optimization, and more. Coding standards, on the other hand, define specific rules and conventions for writing code, ensuring consistency and readability across the codebase.

This guide will explore key best practices and coding standards for JavaScript, focusing on writing clean code, adopting effective design patterns, and maintaining code quality throughout the development lifecycle. By integrating these practices into your workflow, you can enhance the efficiency of your development process and create robust, reliable applications.

.Writing Clean and Maintainable Code

Writing clean and maintainable code is essential for creating software that is not only functional but also easy to understand, debug, and extend. Clean code practices enhance readability, reduce complexity, and facilitate future modifications. Here are key principles to guide you in writing clean and maintainable code:

1. Follow Consistent Naming Conventions

Use meaningful and descriptive names for variables, functions, classes, and other elements. Consistent naming conventions help others (and your future self) understand the purpose and usage of different code components.

Variables: Choose names that clearly describe their purpose (e.g., userAge instead of x).
Functions: Name functions based on their actions or results (e.g., calculateTotalPrice instead of doStuff).
Classes: Use nouns or noun phrases for classes (e.g., InvoiceManager).

2. Write Modular Code

Break down your code into small, reusable modules or functions. Each function should perform a single task or a group of related tasks. This modular approach improves readability and makes it easier to test and maintain your code.

Single Responsibility Principle: Ensure that each function or class has one reason to change.
Avoid Duplication: Reuse code through functions or modules rather than duplicating logic.

3. Keep Functions Short and Focused

Functions should be concise and focused on a single task. Long functions can be difficult to read and understand. Aim for functions that are easy to comprehend and maintain.

Limit Function Length: If a function exceeds a certain length, consider refactoring it into smaller helper functions. Descriptive Parameters: Use parameters that clearly indicate their purpose.

4. Use Clear and Concise Comments

While clean code should minimize the need for comments, use them to clarify complex logic, explain the purpose of functions, or provide context where necessary. Avoid redundant comments that restate what the code is doing.

Why, Not What: Explain why the code is doing something, not just what it is doing.
Update Comments: Ensure comments are kept up to date with code changes.

5. Adopt Consistent Formatting

Consistent code formatting enhances readability and makes it easier to follow the code. Use a style guide or code formatter to maintain consistency in indentation, spacing, and bracket placement.

Indentation: Follow a consistent indentation style (e.g., 2 spaces, 4 spaces).
Line Length: Limit line length to improve readability (e.g., 80-120 characters).

6. Handle Errors Gracefully

Implement error handling to manage unexpected situations and improve the robustness of your code. Use try-catch blocks, validation checks, and proper logging to handle and report errors.

Catch Specific Errors: Handle specific error types rather than using generic error handling.
Provide Meaningful Messages: Ensure error messages are informative and helpful for debugging.

7. Write Tests for Your Code

Develop unit tests and integration tests to verify the functionality of your code and catch issues early. Testing helps ensure code reliability and supports future changes and refactoring.

Test Coverage: Aim for high test coverage to cover different aspects of your code.
Automate Testing: Use automated testing tools to streamline the testing process.

8. Refactor Regularly

Regularly refactor your code to improve its structure and readability. Refactoring involves making changes to the code without altering its external behavior to enhance maintainability and performance.

Code Reviews: Conduct code reviews to identify areas for improvement and ensure adherence to best practices.
Continuous Improvement: Embrace feedback and continuously seek ways to enhance your code.

Conclusion

Writing clean and maintainable code involves adhering to consistent naming conventions, modularizing code, keeping functions short, using clear comments, formatting consistently, handling errors gracefully, testing thoroughly, and refactoring regularly. By following these principles, you can create code that is easier to read, understand, and maintain, ultimately leading to more efficient development and higher-quality software.

Code Organization and Modularization

Effective code organization and modularization are crucial for creating scalable, maintainable, and understandable software. By structuring code into well-defined modules and following systematic organization practices, developers can improve code readability, facilitate collaboration, and simplify future enhancements. Here's an overview of how to achieve effective code organization and modularization:

1. Modular Design
Modular design involves breaking down your codebase into distinct, manageable units or modules, each responsible for a

specific piece of functionality. This approach enhances maintainability and reusability.

Single Responsibility Principle: Each module or function should have one responsibility or purpose. This makes it easier to understand, test, and maintain.

Encapsulation: Hide internal details of a module and expose only necessary interfaces. This reduces dependencies and potential side effects.

2. Organize Code into Logical Units

Organize your code into directories and files that reflect its functionality. This helps in locating and managing code more efficiently.

Group by Feature: Arrange code by features or functionality rather than by file type. For instance, group all related components, services, and styles for a feature in a single directory.

Use Meaningful Names: Name directories and files clearly to indicate their purpose (e.g., userService.js, orderComponent.js).

3. Create Reusable Components

Encapsulate common functionality into reusable components or modules. This reduces code duplication and promotes consistency.

Component-Based Architecture: In frameworks like React, Vue, and Angular, break down the UI into reusable components that manage their own state and rendering.
Utility Modules: Extract commonly used functions or utilities into separate modules (e.g., dateUtils.js, apiHelpers.js).

4. Implement a Consistent Structure

Adopt a consistent project structure to facilitate navigation and collaboration. Following a standard layout helps new developers get up to speed quickly and maintains a uniform codebase.

Typical Project Structure:
src/: Main source code directory.
components/: Reusable UI components.
services/: Modules for business logic and data handling.
utils/: Utility functions and helpers.
styles/: CSS or styling files.

views/: Higher-level components representing different application views.

public/: Static files such as images and HTML templates.

tests/: Unit and integration tests.

5. Use Dependency Injection

Incorporate dependency injection to manage dependencies between modules and services. This improves flexibility and testing by allowing modules to be easily substituted or mocked.

Constructor Injection: Pass dependencies through a constructor.

Service Locator: Use a centralized service locator to resolve dependencies.

6. Apply Separation of Concerns

Ensure that different aspects of your application, such as data management, business logic, and user interface, are separated into distinct modules or layers. This helps in isolating changes and managing complexity.

MVC Pattern: In traditional web applications, separate concerns into Model (data), View (UI), and Controller (business logic).

Service-Oriented Architecture: Structure your application around services that handle specific business logic or data access.

7. Document Your Modules

Document the purpose, usage, and interface of each module to provide clarity for other developers and maintainers. Well-documented code reduces the learning curve and supports easier collaboration.

Code Comments: Include comments to explain complex logic or decisions.

Documentation Files: Create README files or dedicated documentation for modules to outline their functionality and usage.

8. Adopt Code Review Practices

Implement code reviews to ensure that modularization and code organization standards are followed. Peer reviews help identify potential issues and enforce best practices.

Review Checklists: Use checklists to ensure consistency and completeness during code reviews.

Feedback Loop: Incorporate feedback from reviews to continuously improve code organization and modularity.

Conclusion

Code organization and modularization are fundamental to building high-quality, maintainable software. By designing modular components, structuring your project logically, and adhering to best practices, you can create a codebase that is easier to manage, extend, and collaborate on.

Effective modularization not only improves code quality but also enhances development efficiency and supports future growth.

Performance Optimization

Performance optimization is the process of improving the efficiency of an application to ensure it runs smoothly, responds quickly, and handles high loads effectively. It involves various strategies and techniques to enhance code execution, resource management, and overall system performance. Here's an overview of key aspects of performance optimization:

1. Code Efficiency

Efficient code execution is crucial for application performance. Optimize algorithms and data structures to reduce computational complexity.

Algorithm Optimization: Use algorithms with lower time and space complexity. Profile and identify bottlenecks in your code to focus optimization efforts where they will have the most impact.

Efficient Data Structures: Choose data structures that optimize access and modification times based on your application's needs.

2. Minimize Resource Usage

Reducing the consumption of resources such as memory, CPU, and network bandwidth can lead to significant performance improvements.

Memory Management: Implement efficient memory usage practices and monitor for memory leaks. Use profiling tools to detect and address issues related to excessive memory consumption.

CPU Optimization: Avoid blocking operations and use asynchronous programming to keep the application responsive.

3. Reduce Load Times

Improving the speed at which your application loads enhances the user experience. Focus on optimizing asset delivery and network requests.

Asset Optimization: Compress and minify files such as CSS, JavaScript, and images to reduce their size. Use modern formats and tools to improve asset loading times.

Lazy Loading: Load resources only when needed. Implement lazy loading for images and scripts to speed up the initial page load.

4. Improve Network Performance

Efficient network communication helps in faster data transfer and reduces latency.

Content Delivery Networks (CDNs): Use CDNs to distribute content across multiple servers globally, reducing latency and improving load times.
Optimize API Calls: Minimize payload size and reduce the number of API calls by batching requests or using efficient data formats.

5. Enhance Rendering Performance

Rendering performance affects how quickly and smoothly content is displayed to users.

Reduce Layout Reflows: Minimize changes that trigger layout recalculations, such as frequent DOM manipulations or style changes.
Use Hardware Acceleration: Leverage GPU acceleration for animations and transformations to improve rendering performance.

6. Monitor and Profile

Regular monitoring and profiling are essential for identifying and addressing performance issues.

Performance Monitoring Tools: Utilize tools like browser developer tools, performance analyzers, and real-user monitoring (RUM) tools to track and measure performance metrics.
Profiling: Profile your application to detect bottlenecks, memory leaks, and inefficient code paths. Use profiling data to guide optimization efforts.

7. Optimize Database Interactions

Efficient database interactions are key to application performance, especially for data-intensive applications.

Query Optimization: Write optimized queries and use indexing to speed up data retrieval. Avoid complex joins and ensure efficient database schema design.
Caching: Implement caching strategies to reduce the load on the database and speed up data access.

8. Adopt Best Practices

Adhering to best practices helps in building performant applications from the start.

Code Quality: Write clean, well-structured code and follow best practices for coding and design patterns.
Testing and Validation: Regularly test your application under various conditions to identify performance issues and ensure that optimizations are effective.

Conclusion

Performance optimization is a continuous process that involves improving various aspects of an application, from code efficiency and resource management to network performance and rendering. By applying these strategies and regularly monitoring performance, you can create a faster, more responsive application that delivers a better user experience and handles high loads effectively.

Chapter 16

Deployment and Beyond

Deployment marks the transition of your application from a development environment to a live production environment where it can be accessed by users. However, the deployment process is just the beginning. To ensure the long-term success of your application, it's essential to consider not only the deployment itself but also the ongoing management, monitoring, and optimization that follows.

In this phase, you'll focus on deploying your application efficiently, managing configurations, and setting up environments that support scalability and reliability. Additionally, maintaining the health of your application involves continuous monitoring, troubleshooting issues, and implementing updates or improvements based on user feedback and performance data.

This section will guide you through the deployment process, strategies for managing live environments, and best practices for ensuring your application remains robust, scalable, and responsive to user needs.

Preparing Your Code for Production

Preparing your code for production is a critical step in ensuring that your application performs well, remains secure, and provides a seamless user experience once it is live. This phase involves several key practices and processes to optimize your codebase and deployment strategy. Here's how to effectively prepare your code for production:

1. Optimize Code

Before deploying, review and optimize your code to ensure it runs efficiently in a production environment.

Minify and Bundle: Minify JavaScript, CSS, and HTML files to reduce their size and improve load times. Bundle multiple files into single files to reduce the number of HTTP requests.

Remove Debugging Code: Eliminate console logs, debug statements, and development-specific code that should not be present in the production environment.

2. Enhance Security

Securing your application is crucial to protect it from vulnerabilities and threats.

Sanitize Input: Ensure that all user inputs are validated and sanitized to prevent injection attacks and other security vulnerabilities.
Use HTTPS: Configure your server to use HTTPS for secure data transmission. This helps protect sensitive information from being intercepted.

Update Dependencies: Keep all third-party libraries and dependencies up to date to mitigate security risks associated with outdated versions.

3. Configure Environment Variables

Set up environment-specific configurations to ensure that your application behaves correctly in different environments (development, staging, production).

Separate Configurations: Store environment variables separately for development and production to avoid accidental exposure of sensitive information.
Use Configuration Management Tools: Leverage tools or services to manage environment variables securely and efficiently.

4. Implement Error Handling and Logging

Effective error handling and logging are essential for diagnosing and resolving issues in production.

Error Reporting: Implement robust error handling to capture and report errors. Use tools like Sentry or LogRocket for real-time error tracking and reporting.

Logging: Set up comprehensive logging to monitor application performance and detect issues. Ensure logs are accessible but protected from unauthorized access.

5. Conduct Testing

Perform thorough testing to identify and address any potential issues before deployment.

Unit and Integration Testing: Run unit tests and integration tests to validate that individual components and their interactions work as expected.

Performance Testing: Conduct performance testing to ensure your application can handle expected loads and stress levels without degrading performance.

6. Prepare Deployment Artifacts

Create deployment artifacts that are ready for production.

Build Artifacts: Generate build artifacts (e.g., compiled code, bundled files) that are optimized for performance and ready for deployment.

Documentation: Prepare deployment documentation and instructions to guide the deployment process and ensure consistency.

7. Automate Deployment

Automate the deployment process to minimize manual errors and ensure a smooth release.

Continuous Integration/Continuous Deployment (CI/CD): Set up CI/CD pipelines to automate the build, test, and deployment processes, ensuring that code changes are integrated and deployed consistently.

Deployment Scripts: Use deployment scripts or tools to automate the deployment process and manage different stages of deployment (e.g., staging, production).

8. Monitor and Review

Once your application is live, continuous monitoring and review are essential to maintain its health and performance.

Application Monitoring: Implement monitoring tools to track application performance, uptime, and user interactions. Monitor metrics such as response times, error rates, and resource usage.

Regular Reviews: Conduct regular reviews and audits of your application to identify areas for improvement and ensure ongoing compliance with security and performance standards.

Conclusion

Preparing your code for production involves optimizing and securing your code, configuring environment-specific settings, implementing error handling and logging, and automating the deployment process. By following these best practices, you can ensure a smooth transition to a live environment and maintain the performance, security, and reliability of your application over time.

Hosting and Deployment Options

Choosing the right hosting and deployment options is crucial for ensuring your application runs efficiently, scales effectively, and remains accessible to users. Here's a breakdown of common hosting and deployment options, each with its own advantages and use cases:

1. Shared Hosting
Shared hosting is a cost-effective option where multiple websites share the same server resources.

Advantages:

Cost-Effective: Typically the most affordable hosting option.
Ease of Use: Often includes user-friendly management tools and support.
Disadvantages:
Limited Resources: Shared resources can lead to performance issues during peak times.

Less Control: Limited access to server configurations and customization.

Best For: Small websites and applications with modest traffic and resource needs.

2. Virtual Private Server (VPS) Hosting

.

VPS hosting provides a virtualized server environment with dedicated resources.

Advantages:

.

Greater Control: More control over server configurations and customization.

Scalability: Easier to scale resources compared to shared hosting.

Disadvantages:

Higher Cost: More expensive than shared hosting.

Management Complexity: Requires more technical knowledge for server management.

Best For: Medium-sized applications and websites needing more control and dedicated resources.

3. Dedicated Server Hosting

Dedicated server hosting provides an entire physical server dedicated to your application.

Advantages:

Full Control: Complete control over server configurations and performance.
High Performance: Dedicated resources lead to better performance and reliability.

Disadvantages:

High Cost: Generally the most expensive hosting option.
Complex Management: Requires advanced knowledge for server administration and maintenance.
Best For: Large applications and websites with high traffic and resource demands.

4. Cloud Hosting
.

Cloud hosting uses virtual servers hosted in a cloud environment, providing scalable and flexible resources.

Advantages:

.

Scalability: Easily scale resources up or down based on demand.

High Availability: Redundant systems ensure high uptime and reliability.

Pay-as-You-Go: Pay only for the resources you use, which can be cost-effective.

Disadvantages:

Complex Pricing: Variable pricing can be challenging to predict and manage.

Vendor Lock-In: Potential dependency on specific cloud providers and their services.

Best For: Applications with variable traffic, need for high availability, and scalable resources.

5. Platform-as-a-Service (PaaS)

PaaS provides a platform allowing developers to build, deploy, and manage applications without managing the underlying infrastructure.

Advantages:

Developer Focus: Focus on application development without worrying about infrastructure.
Integrated Services: Access to development tools, databases, and other services.

Disadvantages:

Limited Control: Less control over the underlying infrastructure and environment.
Cost: Can be more expensive than traditional hosting solutions depending on usage.
Best For: Developers who want to streamline the deployment process and focus on application development.

6. Serverless Hosting

Serverless hosting allows you to build and run applications without managing servers. You pay only for the execution time of your code.

Advantages:
Automatic Scaling: Scales automatically based on demand.

Cost Efficiency: Pay only for the actual compute time used.

Disadvantages:

Cold Start Latency: Potential latency for functions that are not frequently invoked.
Complexity in Debugging: Debugging serverless applications can be more challenging.
Best For: Applications with variable workloads and event-driven architectures.

7. Container Hosting

Container hosting involves deploying applications in containers (e.g., Docker), which encapsulate the application and its dependencies.

Advantages:

Portability: Consistent environments across development, testing, and production.
Scalability: Easily scale containers and manage deployments using orchestration tools like Kubernetes.

Disadvantages:

Complexity: Requires knowledge of containerization and orchestration tools.

Overhead: May introduce additional overhead for managing container infrastructure.

Best For: Applications requiring consistent environments, portability, and advanced orchestration.

Conclusion

Selecting the right hosting and deployment options depends on factors such as the size of your application, traffic levels, resource needs, and budget. Whether opting for shared hosting, cloud solutions, PaaS, or serverless hosting, each option has its advantages and trade-offs. Understanding these options helps you make informed decisions to ensure your application performs optimally and meets user expectations.

www.ingramcontent.com/pod-product-compliance
Lightning Source LLC
LaVergne TN
LVHW051429050326
832903LV00030BD/2988